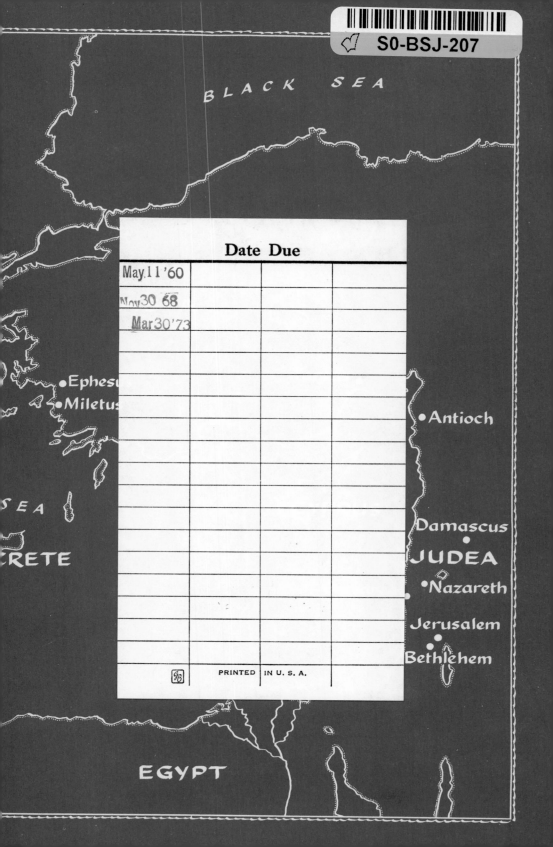

BLACK SEA

Date Due

May.11 '60			
Nov 30 68			
Mar 30'73			
	PRINTED	IN U. S. A.	

Ephesu

Miletus

Antioch

SEA

CRETE

Damascus

JUDEA

Nazareth

Jerusalem

Bethlehem

EGYPT

The Living Story of the New Testament

Books by Walter Russell Bowie

THE STORY OF THE BIBLE

THE STORY OF THE CHURCH

LIFT UP YOUR HEARTS

CHRIST BE WITH ME

THE STORY OF JESUS FOR YOUNG PEOPLE

GREAT MEN OF THE BIBLE

THE MASTER: A LIFE OF JESUS CHRIST

I BELIEVE IN JESUS CHRIST

THE LIVING STORY OF THE NEW TESTAMENT

"I am the light of the world."

THE
LIVING STORY
OF THE
NEW TESTAMENT

by

Walter Russell Bowie

Illustrated by Douglas Rosa

PRENTICE-HALL, INC.
Englewood Cliffs, N.J.

39,174
March, 1960

To

BEVERLEY MUNFORD BOWIE

Brilliant and Beloved

Death hath no dominion over him

Foreword

ONCE there was a life which seemed to end, but did not end. There was a Man who died, but is not dead; who moves today in the world as a power that touches people everywhere and makes them different from what they were before.

When this Man walked the earth, there were other men who seemed to be more important. There were kings and emperors, generals of armies, governors with cruel authority, high-placed and proud. He was like none of those; and most of them never supposed that anything he said or did would matter much. But some of them are forgotten; and those who are not forgotten are remembered chiefly because their names appear in the record of what that One was.

They are a part of history that is dead. But the Man who was above all others is alive in what goes on in the world today. That is why continually there will be new ways, in words and in pictures, of trying to tell about him. And that is why this book, therefore, may be called *The Living Story of the New Testament.*

WALTER RUSSELL BOWIE
Alexandria, Va.

Contents

CHAPTER ONE

The Great Hope

THE LAND of Palestine at the eastern end of the Mediterranean Sea is only a little strip of country, but it has had a long and crowded history. Through the centuries the armies of many nations have crossed its borders on their roads of conquest—armies from Babylonia and Assyria, from Persia and from Egypt, from Greece and Rome, from Arabia and from the newer nations of the West.

Now, in the twentieth century, Jewish people from all quarters of the earth have come back to Palestine and created a new nation which bears the old, old name of Israel. So a new chapter in history begins. But more important than anything else that has happened in Palestine, or that may happen in the future, is what came to pass there more than nineteen hundred years ago.

In those days, as now, Palestine was the homeland of the people of Israel. The Old Testament is the record of their ancient history, and of what they believed God meant them to be among the peoples of the earth. Once they themselves had been a great kingdom. But again and again they had been conquered by other nations who were stronger than they. At last they were held within the mighty empire of Rome, whose armies had marched victorious over far regions of the world. Yet the people of Israel remembered that the prophets, who spoke in the name of God, had promised that some day there would come to them a Savior. They did not know when that would be, or what he would be like, but always the hope was burning.

The New Testament is the story of how that hope was fulfilled, in a way so unexpected that even now our utmost thinking cannot fully comprehend it. There was a life which began in an obscure corner of a little town, and was destroyed—or seemed to be destroyed—upon a cross; yet in *that* life the faith of much of the world has centered. The New Testament begins with the four books called the Gospels, which are the records that were gathered concerning Jesus of Nazareth after he had lived in Palestine; then in the rest of the New Testament are letters and other writings from those who had loved and followed him. In the beginning, too much was happening for anyone to sit down and write, but before long men commenced to put into words what they remembered, and what they heard from others, of him who had been so great that no description of him could be more wonderful than what he was. Who these writers were to whom we owe the different parts of the New Testament, when they wrote, and where and how, can be studied to our vivid interest and profit in commentaries on the Bible. But more important than all else is what they wrote, and it is of this that the pages which follow are to tell.

CHAPTER TWO

The Birth of Jesus

I N THE HILLS of Galilee, in the northern part of Palestine, there was a little town called Nazareth. In Nazareth, at the time from which the year 1 of the world's calendar is now dated, there lived a maiden named Mary, who was young and lovely, and was soon to be married. Mary knew what the prophets of long ago had believed and said, that the time was coming when God would send to his people the One who should be their Savior. But Mary did not know that God had chosen her to be the mother of this One.

Then one day something wonderful happened. To Mary there came a heavenly vision, in which she saw what only eyes lifted up to God could see. There before her stood an angel, tall and beautiful and shining. And this is what he said to her: "Hail, O favored one, the Lord is with you!"

Mary trembled, for who would not tremble to be in the presence of a messenger from God?

But the angel said to her, "Do not be afraid, Mary, for you have found favor with God." And then he went on to tell her that presently she would have a son, and that she should name him Jesus.

"He will be great," the angel said, "and will be called the Son of the Most High. And the Lord God will give him the throne of his father David. He will reign over the house of Jacob forever; and of his Kingdom there will be no end."

But Mary thought, "How can that be?" She was only a

maid of Nazareth. How should she have a son who would be greater than all the kings of earth?

"The Holy Spirit will come upon you, and the power of the Most High will overshadow you," the angel said. "Therefore the child to be born will be called holy, the Son of God."

So Mary bowed before the angel as he spoke to her. "Let it be to me," she said, "according to your word."

Now Mary did not tremble any more, but instead her heart was filled with joy. For the angel, whose name was Gabriel (and Gabriel is the angel believed to stand closest to the glory of God) had told her something else that made her glad. Her cousin Elizabeth was also going to have a son. "I will go to see her!" Mary said to herself.

She rose, and hastened on her way. Down from the hills of Nazareth she went, along the roads that led to the hill country of Judea where Elizabeth lived. And when Elizabeth saw Mary she greeted her with eagerness, and Mary poured out to her the story of the visit of the angel and the promise he had brought.

Then Elizabeth and Mary rejoiced together. "Blessed are you among women," Elizabeth cried. And Mary's heart was so full of wonder and of thankfulness that she could not help but sing. What she sang has come down to us in the hymn called the Magnificat, in the Gospel of Luke—the song of Mary who had formerly thought of herself as only a lowly maiden, but who knew now that:

> "He who is mighty has done great things for me,
> And holy is his name."

As Mary revealed to Elizabeth what had happened in Nazareth, so Elizabeth told what had happened to her. Her husband Zechariah was a priest in the Temple at Jerusalem; and there one day as he stood before the altar in the smoke of the burning incense, an angel had appeared to him.

"Your wife Elizabeth will bear you a son, and you shall call his name John," the angel said. "You shall have joy and gladness, and many will rejoice at his birth."

For the son would grow up, the angel said, to be a prophet— in spirit and power like the great Elijah of Old Testament times—who would "turn many of the sons of Israel to the Lord their God."

But Zechariah could not believe it, for he said he was an old man, and his wife was not young either.

Then said the angel: "I am Gabriel, who stand in the presence of God; and I was sent to speak to you." And now, because Zechariah had not believed the angel's message, he would be unable to speak until the promise was fulfilled.

That was what Mary learned from Elizabeth, and she also learned that Elizabeth's child was surely coming. So both of them were happy when Mary had completed her visit, and set out again for her home in Nazareth.

Time went by, and Elizabeth's son was born. All the friends and neighbors rejoiced with her. Then arose the question of what to name the child. Nearly everybody said he ought to be named Zechariah, after his father. But his mother said no, he should be named John. "Nobody in your family has that name," they all said. Then they asked Zechariah what he thought. Zechariah still could not speak, and so he made signs asking for something to write on. He wrote, "His name is John." Then suddenly Zechariah found that he could talk again, and he began to praise God and to prophesy concerning the sort of man John should grow up to be:

> "Thou, child, shalt be called the prophet of the Most High,
>   for thou shalt go before the Lord to prepare his ways,
>   to give knowledge of salvation to his people . . .
>   in the forgiveness of their sins . . .
>   to give light to those who sit in darkness and in the shadow
>   of death,
>   to guide our feet into the way of peace."

All this was true, as we shall see. For the time would come, after John had grown to be a man, when people by the thousands and tens of thousands would come to listen to him as he stood up and spoke to them of God.

So the birth of John was a great event, but something much greater was to come.

The time was drawing near when the promise which Mary of Nazareth had heard from the angel was to be fulfilled. The word "Gospel" means "good news," and the parts of the Bible which are called the Gospels are the good news that was told with wonder, and later written down, about the birth of Jesus.

Mary was married now to Joseph, and Joseph had to make a journey away from Nazareth. The order had gone out from the Roman rulers that all the men of Israel must go and report their names for taxing, in the towns to which their families had belonged. Now Joseph's family town was Bethlehem, so that was where he had to go.

Mary went with him, though the way was long. Down from the hills of Galilee they journeyed, along the valley of the Jordan River, then up the higher hills past the city of Jerusalem, until at last they came to little Bethlehem. But there were many others also on the road. Night was falling when they reached the gates of Bethlehem, and other travelers who had passed them had gone in before. When they found the inn where they had hoped for warmth and shelter, it was already full. There was no room for them.

Where could they turn then? No house was open. No bed where Mary could lie down. But nearby there was a rough cave which had been made into a stable, and Joseph took Mary there. If there was any warmth, it was only from the bodies of the patient cattle; if any light, only the far light of the stars. But there that night in the stable Mary brought forth her first-born son.

The people who were asleep in Bethlehem did not know.

Neither did the great ones out in the wide world know, or care. What did it matter if there were one child more or less in a tiny Judean town? Far off in Rome, the emperor, Augustus Caesar, dwelt in his palace. Suppose someone had told him that a baby was born in one of the conquered countries over which he ruled. He might have asked scornfully what difference that could make to him. Yet that child born in Bethlehem was more important than Augustus Caesar, or than all the other kings on earth. For Mary's son was Jesus.

Now humble folk can sometimes know when God comes near better than the great and proud can know. That is the reason for the beautiful chapter in the Gospel according to Luke which tells the story of the shepherds. Out in the fields near Bethlehem, guarding their sheep, these shepherds were humble men, and poor. They did not have any great possessions, but that did not keep them from having great thoughts. Bethlehem was the town where long before the young

David had lived, and in those very fields David had kept his father's sheep. It was David who afterwards had gone out to fight the giant Goliath, and after that had become the king of Israel. Those were the glorious days; but had they gone forever? It may be that the shepherds were remembering David, and wondering—as many men did wonder—when the day might come when God would send One mightier even than David to be the Deliverer of his people.

Then suddenly, as they sat about their fire in the wintry night, a great glory shone about them. There in the light, and in the glory of it, was the figure of an angel. And the shepherds were filled with fear.

But the angel said, "Be not afraid."

Then his voice went on: "Behold, I bring you good news of a great joy which will come to all the people; for to you is born this day in the city of David a Savior, who is Christ the Lord. And this will be a sign for you: you will find a babe wrapped in swaddling cloths and lying in a manger."

When he had finished speaking, it seemed to the shepherds as though there were no longer one angel, but a host of angels, who filled the sky with the splendor of their wings. They were singing:

> "Glory to God in the highest,
>   and on earth peace among men with whom he is
>   pleased."

Then again the night was silent, and only the stars shone in the sky.

But the shepherds sprang up with excitement. "Good news of great joy"—that is what had been told them. A child was born in David's town. And he would be Christ the Lord!

"Let us go to Bethlehem and see," they said to one another.

So into Bethlehem they went, until they found the place where Mary and Joseph were. And there they saw the little child Jesus, wrapped in swaddling cloths and lying in a

And the Angel Gabriel came to Mary and said, "Hail, O favored one."

The boy Jesus in Joseph's carpenter shop.

manger, just as the voice of the angel had told them he would be.

Were they filled with wondering then? It might have seemed that this was not the proper way in which One who would be greater than David, and greater than all other kings, would come. That he would have a mother so poor that she had no cradle for her baby except a bed of straw in a manger where cattle fed. Yet God does not depend upon the things which men suppose must belong to those who will be great. So they knelt down, and told what they had seen and heard in their vision of the angels out in the fields where they had left their sheep. And then they went away, praising and glorifying God.

CHAPTER THREE

The Coming of the Magi

NOR WERE the shepherds the only ones who came to see the little Jesus. In another one of the Gospels—the Gospel according to Matthew—there is the story of other men who came from a long way off to find him. For in the Eastern countries there were those who did not belong to the people of Israel, but who had nonetheless heard of the hope of Israel. They had read an ancient writing which said that

> "There shall come forth a star out of Jacob
> And a scepter shall rise out of Israel."

Now these men in the lands of the East had a religion of their own. They believed that everywhere there was a struggle between the power of light and the power of darkness, and that wherever there was light, God was helping men to remember him. Especially they studied the stars, because they thought that in the stars were signs from God. They were called the Magi; and the Gospel of Matthew calls them the Wise Men.

One night the Magi saw in the sky what seemed to them a new star.

"What can it mean?" they asked one another. Could it mean that in the land of Israel there had arisen One who had come from God to bring his message for all the earth? They would go and see.

So they made ready for a long journey, and presently they saddled their camels and set out. Day after day they rode: through the valley between the great rivers, the Tigris and Euphrates; over the long miles of drifting sand and empty desert that lay beyond; past the city of Damascus and its gardens; along the shore of the Lake of Galilee and the Jordan River; and over the hills of Judea until they came at last to Jerusalem, and to the palace of Herod the king.

The Magi were not poor men, as the shepherds were. The Gospel of Matthew tells of rich treasures that they had brought with them; and other stories that afterwards were told about them say that in their own country they were kings, and that their names were Gaspar, Melchior, and Balthazar. So there would be excitement in the court of Herod when their caravan appeared. They seemed important enough for Herod to welcome.

But Herod's welcome could be dangerous. For Herod, whom the Romans had appointed to rule in Jerusalem, was an old man now, suspicious and cruel. In spasms of rage he had put his own wife and one of his sons to death when they roused his jealousy. What, Herod asked himself, had these Magi come for?

He was soon to find out. They entered into the royal hall, these noble looking visitors from afar, where Herod waited to receive them. And when they had saluted Herod, this is what they asked him:

"Where is he who has been born King of the Jews? For we have seen his star in the East, and have come to worship him."

So! They were looking for a king of the Jews—and they meant another king. They knew well enough that Herod was king of the Jews already. Then what they were saying was that someone else should be king instead. That was treason!

To Herod this was what their words must mean, and his heart was furious. But he would not let his face betray what he was feeling. He would pretend to help these Magi.

Herod called for some of those at his court who knew the writings of the prophets. He demanded to know what they could find there about anyone who would be born king of the Jews.

They told him that long ago the prophet Micah had declared that the time was coming when God himself would send a ruler over Israel, and that he would be born in Bethlehem.

Then Herod said to the Magi, "Go and search diligently for the child. When you have found him, bring me word. And I will come and worship him too." That is what he said, though what he meant was something very different.

Yet the Magi rejoiced because they knew now where to go. They mounted their camels again and rode to Bethlehem. Through the gate of the little town they came, and along its street until they found where the child Jesus lay. And entering the house, they opened the treasures which they had brought, and laid down their gifts of gold and frankincense and myrrh.

Then they remembered how Herod had told them that if they found the child they were to let him know, so that he, too, could come and worship him. But it may have been that they had seen in Herod's eyes the evil purpose that he could not hide. And that night they dreamed of Herod, and when they saw him in their dream they were sure it was not safe to have anything more to do with him. So they went home to their own country by another way.

For a while Herod waited. Then he began to know that the Magi were not going to do what he had told them. He was hot with anger to think that he had been outwitted. He did not know exactly where the child he feared might be, or which child in Bethlehem he was. But he would take no chances about him. No child would grow up to be king of the Jews if Herod could help it. So the Gospel of Matthew says that he called the commander of his soldiers. He told him to go to Bethlehem and to kill every young male child he could find.

Then to Bethlehem Herod's soldiers came. What had been the quiet street of the little town was filled with noise and sudden terror: the heavy feet of soldiers running, the smash-

ing in of doors, the screams and pleadings of mothers as they clutched their babies to their breasts. But Herod's troops were merciless, and when they marched away they left only death behind them, and the sound of women weeping for the children who had been slain.

But Jesus was not among them. Before Herod had sent his soldiers out, Joseph had had a dream which warned him that there might be danger. So he had taken Mary and Jesus, and they had fled—the tradition handed down in Matthew's Gospel says—to Egypt.

CHAPTER FOUR

Jesus Growing Up in Nazareth

HEROD's last cruelty had failed. Jesus was alive; and soon Herod himself, an old man, evil and full of hate, was dead.

Herod's son, Archelaus, took his place. He was a man much like his father, so it was not safe to go into Judea where he reigned. But Nazareth, in Galilee, was not part of the country over which Archelaus ruled. So it was safe now for Joseph, with Mary and the little Jesus, to go home.

Nazareth was a village in the hills. Life was quiet and simple there, but reminders of the great world outside were not far away. Over the hills lay the Lake of Galilee, busy with its fishing boats. On its shores were new cities which the Romans had built. Up and down the roads not far from Nazareth moved the caravans, long lines of shuffling camels laden with the goods that were carried in the trade between Egypt and the countries across the desert to the east—woolen cloths and linen, dates and figs and grain, cinnamon and sandalwood, perfumes and spices, and ivory and gold. On the roads, too, a company of Roman soldiers might be marching, their gilded eagles, which they carried instead of flags, glinting in the sun. And from the tops of the highest hills there could be seen in the distance the blue water of the Mediterranean Sea, where great galleys, propelled by banks of oars when the wind was not in the sails, made Rome able to control the sea as her armies controlled the land.

There in Nazareth Jesus was to live until he was grown. The signs of Roman power were all about, but Rome was not the power that the men of Nazareth recognized in their hearts. They belonged to the people of Israel, and they believed that they were the Chosen People of God. In the part of the Bible that is the Old Testament they read of their long history. Once their nation had seemed great, and they believed that God would make it great again.

Sometimes the impatience and anger which men felt because the Romans ruled their country grew greater than they could bear. Only a few miles from Nazareth was the city of Sepphoris. There, when Jesus was still a little boy, hatred against the Romans flamed into a war. Men who wanted freedom took possession of the city. But the Roman general Varus, with his troops, laid siege to Sepphoris. They broke down its gates, fought through its streets, and killed many of those who tried to defend it. Then they set Sepphoris on fire. And as for those of the defenders who were taken alive, they were not carried off to prison. Instead, the Romans nailed them up on crosses along the roads. It may be that Jesus saw the flames of burning Sepphoris and the men who were crucified, and already was beginning to be sure that fighting and killing were not what God meant for his people.

Certainly he was thinking often of God. In every Jewish family the mother and father would teach a child as soon as he was old enough to listen and understand. It would be Mary first, telling the little boy the wonderful stories written in the Bible: of how God made the heavens and the earth; of the Garden of Eden and the angel with the flaming sword; of Noah and how God taught him to build the ark to save his family and the animals when the great flood came; of how God

called Abraham from the far country; of how Joseph was sold
into Egypt; and of Moses, hidden in the reeds by the river
where the princess found him; of the little boy Samuel,
brought by his mother to help the old priest Eli in the Temple; and of David, the shepherd lad who slew Goliath. And
as Mary sang to him when he was sleepy, she may have sung
to him the lovely verses of the psalms.

When Jesus was a little older, Joseph would take him with
him to the synagogue on the Sabbath Day. That was where
the whole village went to church, to hear the Word of God
and to join in the same beautiful prayers and praises that the
people of Israel had offered up since hundreds of years before.
And it was not only in the synagogue and on the sabbath that
God was remembered. On the door post of every Jewish home
there was a tiny metal case called the Mezuzah, and in it was a
little roll on which was written the Bible words:

> "Hear, O Israel: the Lord our God is one Lord:
> And thou shalt love the Lord thy God with all thine heart,
> and with all thy soul, and with all thy might."

Whenever anyone went in or out by the door, he would
touch the Mezuzah with his fingers and remember the words
that were written there.

So also when mealtime came, Joseph would offer thanks to
God for the food they were about to have:

> "Blessed art thou, O Lord our God, King of the Universe,
> who bringest forth bread from the earth."

And at special periods of the year, there would be the feasts
that carried on the memory of the great deeds that God had
done for his people in the long history of Israel. One was the
Feast of Lights, which told again of how the holy Temple in
Jerusalem had been cleansed after one of the heathen conquerors had set up heathen worship there. On the first night

a lamp was lighted, and on the second night another lamp, and so on each night until at the end of the week the whole house would be bright. And in the springtime there would be the holiest feast of all, the Passover. When the family sat down to eat the roasted lamb and the bread, Jesus, as the oldest son, would ask what this festival meant; and Joseph, answering, would tell of the first Passover, and of how their fathers ate it in haste long ago on the night before Moses led the people of Israel out of slavery in Egypt and over the Red Sea into the Promised Land.

The family in Nazareth was growing. Four little boys came, whose names were James and John and Simon and Judah, and at least two sisters, whose names we do not know. And we may think of Jesus as the brother to whom the little ones looked up.

If we ask what Jesus did in Nazareth, the Gospels do not tell us. But we can guess, and have good reason to think the guess is right, because we know what life was like in the villages of Galilee, and because in what Jesus later talked about we can trace his memories of the Nazareth days. Like all the other boys in a Jewish village, he went to the synagogue school, where long passages from the Bible were learned by heart and recited aloud. As a little child, he would go with his mother when she went to draw water from the village well; and at home he would watch her as she kneaded the yeast into the bread, or as she mended the clothes when they were torn. When he was bigger, he could go to Joseph's shop, for Joseph was a carpenter. There Jesus could learn to help him as he made yokes for oxen and ploughs, or help to smooth the beams for the door posts of some new house that was being built.

In the springtime he could watch men sowing seed in the fields, or perhaps go with some of the shepherds as they led their flocks to pastures in the hills. He saw how sometimes a single sheep would wander away and be lost, and how the shepherd would look everywhere and never rest until he found it. And long afterwards he said that the love of God is like that. If any one of God's children sins and goes astray, God will seek for him to bring him home.

CHAPTER FIVE

The Passover in Jerusalem

TIME went by, and Jesus was twelve years old. That was the time when a boy in Israel began to be treated as a man. He could take part now in all the holiest worship; and above all, instead of keeping the Passover at home in Nazareth, he could go up to Jerusalem itself.

Hardly anything could be as exciting as that! Jerusalem was the Holy City—for all the people of Israel the city of their pride and hope. David, the king, had made Jerusalem his capital a thousand years before. Solomon, his son, had built the first great temple there. More men than anyone could know had died to defend Jerusalem when enemy armies marched against it. Once it had been destroyed, its walls torn down, its houses set on fire, and its people carried off as captives. But even then they never forgot the city they loved. In spite of their captivity, no matter how far away they were, their thoughts turned back. "By the rivers of Babylon we sat down and wept when we remembered," they sang in one of the mourning psalms. But still they kept their faith that mourning would not be the last word. Jerusalem would be built again.

And it *had* been built again. Best of all, the Temple had been built again. It was more splendid now than it had ever been before. It stood on its vast stone foundations on the crest of a hill, shining and magnificent. Its lofty walls and long rows of carved pillars were of marble, and its great doorways, and even the roof of its inmost shrine, were covered with gold.

This was the Temple to which the worshippers went up at Passover time. From Nazareth many of the neighbors would be going, and the only way most of them had to get there was to walk. Joseph and Mary took Jesus, and they set out with the others. It was a happy pilgrimage, for it was in the spring, and the hills and fields were bright with flowers after the winter rains. Families and friends walked together in the daytime, and slept out under the stars at night. From the hills of Galilee the way led across the beautiful plain of Esdraelon, down the valley of the Jordan River, and up the steep road that led from the river toward Jerusalem. Then, after three or four days' journey, they reached the top of the Mount of Olives; and there on its height across from them was Jerusalem, with the Temple rising glorious against the sky. No wonder they burst into singing.

> "As the mountains are round about Jerusalem,
>   So the Lord is round about his people from henceforth
>   even for ever."

That was the way Jesus first saw the Holy City. But what he most wanted to see and to go into was the Temple, where God had been worshipped for hundreds and hundreds of years.

At length the Passover was finished, and Mary and Joseph were ready to go home. They did not see Jesus when they started out. Yet they did not miss him at first, because they thought he was with some of their friends who were also setting out on the road to Nazareth. But as the day went on, they saw that they were mistaken. He was not there. They inquired among the neighbors, Had anyone seen him? But no one had.

Then they were frightened. Back they went as quickly as they could to Jerusalem. They looked for him in the places in the city where they thought he might be. They searched through the streets. Then they went up to the Temple.

In one of the courts of the Temple, wise old men who loved to study the law of God used to meet to talk together and to answer questions that the people gathering round would ask them. There in their midst, listening and asking his own questions, was Jesus.

Mary and Joseph felt their hearts leap up with thankfulness to see him. But they could not help remembering the worry Jesus had caused them. There was annoyance in his mother's voice when she said to him, "Son, what made you treat us so? Your father and I have been looking for you in distress."

But Jesus lifted his eyes to her in wonder, as though he was surprised that she did not understand. "Didn't you know," he said, "that I must be in my Father's house?"

And the Gospel of Luke says, "His mother kept all these things in her heart." She remembered now that this son of hers had something in his mind and soul that was greater than she could know. He did not belong to her only. He belonged to God.

They went back then to Nazareth, and the Gospel says that "Jesus increased in wisdom and in stature, and in favor with God and man." That is, he grew taller and wiser, and was loved both by God and by the people round him.

CHAPTER SIX

John the Baptist, and the Baptism of Jesus

AFTER the Passover in Jerusalem when Jesus was twelve years old, Joseph is not spoken of in the Gospels again. It seems that some time in the years following he must have died. This meant that Jesus was the head now of his mother's family. He would carry on in the carpenter's shop where Joseph had made a living for them all.

So in the little town Jesus went quietly about his work, as the years went by, until he was almost thirty. It might have seemed that nothing important was happening to him. Out in the great world the power of Rome was still increasing. When the emperor, Augustus Caesar, died it was said of him that he had found Rome a city of brick, and that he had left it magnificently built of marble. Now there was a new emperor, Tiberius. Archelaus, Herod's son, had been removed as king in Jerusalem, and governors were sent instead from Rome to rule there. When Tiberius spoke, Roman armies over half the world carried out his commands. What could come out of Nazareth that would matter in comparison with him? But the answer was that Jesus came, and he was to be more important than any emperor.

In the fifteenth year of Tiberius' reign, there was excitement down by the Jordan River. A man in rough clothes, who looked and spoke with the terrible authority of the prophets of Old Testament times, was preaching to great crowds who flocked to hear him. Who should it be but Jesus' cousin, John, the son of Zechariah and Elizabeth? He said the Kingdom of God was about to come, and that men had better get ready for it. Things they had trusted in and boasted about would not count with God. Only a new goodness in their hearts would count with him. "The ax is laid to the root of the trees," John said; "every tree therefore that does not bear good fruit is cut down and thrown into the fire."

People gazed at him, standing there tall and gaunt in his coat made of camel's skin with a leather belt about his waist, and they trembled at his burning words. What, they asked him, should they do to escape the judgment? And he answered them in plain words. They should stop being dishonest, stop being greedy, stop being cruel.

That is what he said to the ordinary people who knew what they had to be ashamed of. But he had more blistering words for those who thought they were good already. Some of the men who were in high positions in the Jewish religion came down from Jerusalem to find out what he was saying.

"You swarm of snakes!," he cried to them. "Who warned you to flee from the wrath to come?" It was no use for them to think that somehow they had inherited goodness because their forefathers had been good. "Do not presume to say to yourselves," he said, "that 'we have Abraham as our father'; for I tell you, God is able from these stones to raise up children to Abraham." And it was no use for them to pretend to be religious just because they were busy about religious things. They had better look into their own hearts and see the sins they needed to repent of.

When men wanted to repent, John told them that they

should be baptized. He took them into the river where the water that flowed over them would be a sign of God's answer to their prayer that God would wash away their sins. So, because John baptized them, the people called him John the Baptist.

The Kingdom of God was about to come: that was what John was preaching. How would it come? And what would it be like? Those were the questions about which the people wondered.

Some thought that there would be a terrible sign from heaven. The power of God would destroy the heathen peoples, and give the earth to those who had been baptized. And the Messiah would come, for that was what the prophets long ago had promised: the Messiah, or the Christ, the one whom God would send to be the Leader and Deliverer of his people. There were many who believed that when the Messiah appeared, he would come as a conqueror for the sake of Israel only, and would bring vengeance on all the nations that had been Israel's foes. He would "rule with a rod of iron, and break his enemies in pieces."

Men who listened to John there by the Jordan River began to think that here already might be the Promised One. "What do you say about yourself?" they asked him. "Are you the Christ?"

But John answered, "No."

Who *was* John then? Was he Elijah, that great and terrible prophet, come back to earth again? No, he was not Elijah. He was not interested in giving himself a great name. What mattered was that he had come to make people look for the One who would be greater than himself. He said: "I am the voice of one crying in the wilderness, 'Make straight the way of the Lord.' "

The news of what John was doing and saying came to Nazareth. Jesus heard of it. He would go down now to where John was.

Ever since the time when he had gone with Mary and Joseph to the Passover in Jerusalem, Jesus had been thinking of the Kingdom of God, and of what God would have it be. Always it was in his mind and heart. He understood its meaning as neither John nor anyone else could understand it. It would not come with violence. It would mean a new kind of world in which the knowledge of God and the love of God would rule everything that people thought and did. It would

Jesus goes with his parents to his first Passover in Jerusalem.

And Jesus said to them, "Follow me."

be wider than any empire of Rome, and all nations could belong to it. It would be the end of wars and fighting. And it would come most surely not through fear of punishment, as John was preaching, but through the mercy of God which would save those who could not save themselves.

When Jesus came to the Jordan where John was preaching and baptizing, he said that he too would be baptized. Because John had grown up in a different part of the country, it seems that he had never seen Jesus before, and did not know him when he saw him now. But something in the look of Jesus was so great and beautiful that John exclaimed, "I need to be baptized by you, and yet do you come to me?"

But Jesus said that this was the way it should be. He would be baptized with the rest of the people, to show that he joined with them as they came to express their need for God. Though he had not sinned, he would make himself the companion of the sinful. Though he already knew God as no one else could know him, he would stand at the side of the ignorant and the lost.

And when he was baptized, something tremendous happened. As he looked up, he beheld the heavens opened, and the Spirit of God hovering over him like the wings of a dove. And he heard a Voice that said, "Thou art my beloved Son!"

CHAPTER SEVEN

The Temptation in the Wilderness

FROM the moment of his baptism, Jesus knew what perhaps had been coming to him little by little through the quiet years in Nazareth—the truth of what his Father in heaven meant for him to be. *He* was the One to whom the prophets had looked forward. He would be the Messiah and the Savior.

Then, in the Gospels, there is a strange sentence. Jesus had just heard the Voice which had said, "Thou art my beloved Son." But then comes this: "Immediately the spirit drove him out into the wilderness." Is that what God would do? Did he mean to take the One he loved and send him out into a wilderness?

Yes, that is what God did with Jesus. And when we think about it truly, we can see that it was not strange. For what it meant was that Jesus had been entrusted now with a work so great that he must search his mind and fix his purpose in order to be ready for it. He must wrestle with hard questions. And so he must go out into a lonely place to think and pray.

Up into the barren hills he went, and there, as the Gospels tell, he was "tempted by the devil." That is to say, there came into his mind the different ways in which he might use his life. Which would be God's way? That was what he had to determine. Suppose the answer was not clear? And the meaning of

being "tempted by the devil" is that there may always come the satanic voice that tries to keep the way of God from seeming clear, suggesting instead some smooth and selfish choice which pretends to be better and more sensible.

Days went by as Jesus, alone in the wilderness, thought and prayed. Also, he was fasting. At length he realized that he was very hungry. Then came the first word of the devil tempting him. It said that thinking and praying might be all very well, but that the most important thing was to get something to eat. On the barren hillside were loose stones. "Command these stones to become loaves of bread," said the tempting voice.

That temptation meant even more than it might seem. Jesus was hungry. But after his baptism and the words that had come to him from God he was not thinking first of himself. He remembered how many people there were who were nearly always hungry; poor people who had to pay heavy taxes to the Roman rulers, who had to work hard to make a scanty living, who often did not know where their next meal would come from. He was to be sent out now to be the promised Deliverer from God. What better thing could he do than help the hungry to be fed? Suppose this was what God meant him first of all to do—to call on the power of God to satisfy the needs of his own body, and the needs of all God's children who did not have enough to eat.

Certainly if he could do that, he would be comfortable himself; and when he went out presently to preach, people would flock to him because he would be giving them what they thought they wanted most.

Instead Jesus answered the tempting voice:

"It is written,
Man shall not live by bread alone
but by every word that proceeds from the mouth of God."

Bread is important, yes. To feed the body is something everyone has to be concerned with. But it must not crowd out what is more important still. Too many people think of their appetites first, and that is what the devil wanted Jesus to let everybody do. But Jesus knew better. To be bent only upon getting food can make men forget their souls. For himself, there in the wilderness, Jesus could keep on being hungry until he had finished his thinking and his praying. And when he went out presently to teach the people, he must make them also know that the life God has to give them depends upon something more important than what they have to eat.

Then came the second temptation. This is the way it is told in the Gospel:

"The devil took him up, and showed him all the kingdoms of the world in a moment of time, and said to him 'To you I give all this authority and their glory; for it has been delivered to me, and I give it to whom I will. If you, then, will worship me, it shall all be yours.' "

This was the temptation that many of Jesus' own people of Israel would have wanted him to accept. "Authority and glory"—that is what they longed for. Once their nation had amounted to something among the nations of the earth. Now with a fierce resentment they saw that Rome had conquered nearly all the kingdoms of the earth. But always there was the hope that the Messiah would come, and why should not the Messiah be a leader of armies that would make Israel glorious again?

Jesus knew all this. He had thought of it long before. He knew that the rule of Rome was often cruel. Would the world not be better off if the Roman power were broken? Suppose that by the power which God could give him he could smash the Roman empire and set up a new Kingdom in the name of God.

Yes, but to do that he would have to use the same means that Rome had used: violence and hate and war. That is what was meant by the devil showing to his imagination all the kingdoms of the world, and the tempting voice saying to him, "If you will worship me, it shall all be yours"—which was the same as if it had said, "Do as I tell you. You must have power first if people are to listen to you. And you can get power only if you get it my way."

But Jesus knew that this was false. The devil's ways may seem to give power, but that power does not last. Evil can seem to build kingdoms, but afterwards they crumble. The only kingdom Jesus wanted to build was the Kingdom of God, and that Kingdom is built in men's hearts only by love and goodness. So to the temptation he gave his answer:

> "It is written
> 'You shall worship the Lord your God,
> and him only shall you serve.' "

But there was one more temptation still to come.

Jesus now had chosen for himself the way of God, instead

of other ways which might have been easier and more promising. It seemed that there were no more temptations left for the devil to make. But the voice of evil can be very clever, and it can often be most dangerous at the time when it seems that danger is past.

It was as though the devil said to Jesus, "Very well, I leave you now. There is nothing more that I can do to tempt you. You belong to God, and I have no hold upon you. So you can expect from God everything you want. Yes, you have a right to ask anything you choose from him, and he must grant it. No harm can happen to you. If you went up yonder to one of the towers of the Temple and leaped off into the air, you would not fall. For is it not written, "He will give his angels charge of you, to guard you," and "On their hands they will bear you up."

How smooth and right that sounded! But Jesus saw the evil in it. For what the devil wanted was to persuade Jesus that he should make a bargain with God. And God's end of the bargain would be that no great hardship or hurt would come to Jesus. All his way would be smooth and safe.

But Jesus in his strength and courage would have none of that. He knew that to serve God would mean many risks. In the world as it was, he would have to dare and to suffer. The angels of God might or might not be sent to guard him. He would be faithful, whatever happened; and he would not make conditions. He said "It is written, You shall not tempt the Lord your God." By which he meant that he would not say to God, "My Father, I will obey you, *on condition* that you keep me safe."

Now the devil knew indeed that he had been defeated in his last temptation. And Jesus came back from the wilderness so full of gladness and of power that it is no wonder that "angels came and ministered to him."

CHAPTER EIGHT

Jesus Begins His Ministry

FROM the Jordan River Jesus went back to Galilee, his own country. "The Kingdom of God is at hand," he said. "Repent, and believe in the gospel."

"Believe in the gospel." None of the people who heard those words at first could know all that they would come to mean, for no one could see ahead to what would happen in the life of Jesus, and at its end. They would have much to learn before they could understand "the power of God and the wisdom of God" that had come into the world in him. But there was one thing that all the people who listened to Jesus did know. They knew that the gospel they listened to was "good news." When Jesus spoke to them of God he made their hearts grow warm with the feeling that God cared for them.

Jesus loved people, and when he looked at them they knew he loved them. Their neighbors round them might see them only for what they were: men and women with many faults. But Jesus saw them for what they were meant to be: sons and daughters of their Father in heaven. He said one day "I am come that they might have life, and have it more abundantly." They had not learned yet how to live. But if they let God come into their hearts their whole world could be different.

It was no wonder that people wanted to know Jesus and to get close to him. When he returned from the Jordan Valley and his baptism and temptation, he came one day along the shore of the beautiful blue lake of Galilee. Four men were on the water in their fishing boats. Two of them Jesus had seen before, down by the Jordan River where John had been baptizing. One of them was named Andrew. He had gone off and called his brother Simon, who also had come down to hear John preach, and both of them had kept as near Jesus that day as they could. Jesus had told Simon that he should have a new name: Peter, which meant "a Rock." Now here they were, Simon Peter and Andrew, back in Galilee, and on the lake where they made their living catching and selling fish.

Jesus stopped on the shore and called to them. "Follow me," he said, "and I will make you fishers of men." Probably they did not have very much idea of exactly what he meant by that, but they were so glad to see him that they tumbled out of their boats and came ashore. The one thing they did know was that they wanted to be with him more than they wanted anything else. And they were not the only ones. In another boat were two friends of theirs, named James and John. Jesus called them too. Their father Zebedee was also in the boat, together with some hired men. James and John said to them, "You take care of the boat; we must go." And onto the shore they came, as Andrew and Simon had done, and went with Jesus.

These were the first four men who were to be Jesus' disciples—and "disciple" means a learner. They would be Jesus' companions as he went through Galilee preaching and teaching. Little by little they would learn what the Kingdom of God could be, and how men could enter into it; and later on, as he gave them work to do, they would know what he meant when he said that they should be "fishers of men."

The town by the lake where Peter and Andrew and James and John lived was Capernaum, and in Capernaum there was a synagogue. On the Sabbath Day Jesus went to the service there, and the leader of the synagogue asked him to preach to the people. He did; and the congregation listened to him, hushed and wondering. They said to one another that they had never heard anything like this before. They were familiar with teachers and preachers who could get up and talk about what was written in the Scriptures—who knew them well enough, but who seemed to be saying things at second-hand. But Jesus was different. "He speaks with authority," said the people in the synagogue. Here was a message about God that came straight out of Jesus' heart and out of his own great certainty.

And if the people were impressed that day by what Jesus told them of the love of God, they were still more impressed by what they saw him do. In the synagogue there was a man who was out of his mind. It was as though an evil spirit had got into him to drive out his own senses and to fill him with wild insanity. He cried out and made a disturbance. But Jesus turned to him. He spoke to the wildness in the man. "Be still," he said, "and come out of him." And suddenly, with a shriek, all that was tormenting the man's mind left him. He stood there before Jesus, quieted and healed.

Nor was this the end of what happened on that first Sabbath Day in Capernaum. From the synagogue Jesus went to the house where Peter and Andrew lived. Peter's wife's mother was sick in bed with a fever, and they told Jesus about her. He went in where she was, took her hand, and lifted her up. Instantly the fever left her, and she came in and helped to get the dinner.

All Capernaum was excited. Hearing what had happened in the synagogue and in Peter's house, a crowd of sick people came together that evening in the street. Some of them could walk, and some were carried by their friends. Jesus went out among them. A great pity stirred in his heart, as it always did when he saw anyone in trouble. If he pitied them, he knew that God pitied them too. And the power of God could help them. So he laid his hands on them and blessed them, and many who were sick with all sorts of diseases were healed, and they went away rejoicing.

There even came to him a man who had one of the most dreaded of all diseases, leprosy. When a man had leprosy, his skin turned white and began to fall off, together with some of the flesh; and presently his hands and his feet became so that he could not use them. People were afraid that the lepers' disease would spread to them, and they would drive them away whenever they saw them coming near. So lepers had to go off and live in misery by themselves, crying out "Unclean, unclean!" to warn those who might be approaching on the road.

But this leper came running up to Jesus, and dropped on his knees in front of him. "If you will," he said, "you can make me clean." Jesus stretched out his hand and touched him. "I will," he said. "Be clean." And as the man looked at himself, he saw that the awful look of his skin was changing and he sprang up and went away, crying out to everyone that he was healed.

When the news went out about the leper, so many people flocked to where Jesus was that there was hardly room for them in the town. Jesus went out into the open country, and even there the crowds came looking for him. Then they heard that he had come back again into Capernaum, and they followed to the house where he was, and pressed so thick about him that no one else could get as far as the door.

Now there was a man who was paralyzed, and even if there had been no crowd he could not have gone himself to Jesus. But he had some friends who were determined to help him. They picked him up in his bed clothes and carried him to the house that was surrounded by the crowd. They could not get near the door, but they were not stopped by that. They climbed up on the flat roof and made an opening in it: with

ropes they let the paralyzed man down right in front of Jesus.

"My son," said Jesus, "your sins are forgiven."

Some of the men who crowded round him in the house were shocked when they heard him say that. "This is blasphemy," they whispered. "Who can forgive sins but God himself?" The Gospel calls these men "the scribes." They were learned in the Scriptures and thought they knew all about the ways of God. But Jesus understood more than they had ever learned. "The Son of man," he said, "has authority on earth to forgive sins."

This was the first time that Jesus used of himself this name, "the Son of man." The scribes remembered that in the Book of the prophet Daniel the Savior who would come from God had been called "the Son of man." But they were not ready to believe that Jesus was anyone such as that. So they looked at him in sullen anger.

All the same, they were to see that in Jesus the power of God was working, whether they wanted to recognize it or not.

Jesus turned to the paralyzed man. He had already said to him what mattered most—that his sins were forgiven. By this pronouncement he had lifted from the man the load of his fear that he might be so worthless that God might not care for him.

Now Jesus said to him: "Rise, take up your bed and go home." Instantly a great new strength flowed into this man who had been paralyzed. He got up, as Jesus said he could, rolled up the bed mat on which he had been let down, and went out through the astonished crowd. No wonder the Gospel says that "they were all amazed and glorified God, saying, 'We never saw anything like this!'"

CHAPTER NINE

Men Who Would Not Listen

B UT THOUGH the people in general thanked God for Jesus, the number of those who watched him suspiciously was growing. There were first "the scribes," the stubborn men who would not believe that God would show himself in any ways except those they had read about in their books.

And there were also those known as "the Pharisees." Now the Pharisees were men who were supposed to be more religious than all the rest of the people. And it was true that they did have a great history. About two hundred years before, the Jewish nation had gone through a terrible time. A heathen king named Antiochus had sent his armies into the land of Israel to conquer it; and he knew that the only way to keep it conquered would be to stamp out the religion that made the Jews the kind of people they were. So he had set up a heathen altar in the Temple at Jerusalem. He ordered that every copy of the Scriptures should be hunted out and destroyed. He thought that if the Jews could no longer worship God, no longer go up to the Temple and keep their holy days, and no longer have even the Scriptures in which they could read what God had taught their fathers through Moses and the prophets, then the spirit of the people would be broken— they would be no different from the ordinary nations round about. Antiochus was right in what he thought; for it was their faith in God and in God's will for them, and only this, that made the Jewish people strong and resolute enough to stand up against him. The only way he could make them surrender would be to break down their religion.

This was where the Pharisees came in. They were the men who were determined that no matter what persecution and suffering they had to face, they would never let the religion of Israel be destroyed. They fought to keep their copies of the Scriptures. They read them, and they lived by what they read. Here was the Word of God, and they would be faithful to it in spite of every danger, and to the death.

But the trouble was that, as time went on, the Pharisees had lost the right idea of what God's word really meant. They forgot that what God cares about are the big things, such as being brave and generous, and merciful and kind. Instead, they got the idea that religion must be made up of a thousand little rules—rules such as whom you should associate with, and what kind of food you should eat, and what you could do on one day but not on another. When they saw what Jesus did, they were annoyed because he seemed to them to be always breaking these rules.

One day they saw him go to dinner with people who did not pay attention to all their strict ideas. Why didn't Jesus keep to respectable company, they wanted to know, instead of letting himself be seen with the rag, tag, and bobtail of the town?

Jesus answered them. He said of course he would go to these people whom the Pharisees looked down on and called sinners. That was what he had come for. People who were good already —or who thought they were—might not need him. But people who admitted that they were sinners did need him. A doctor does not go to well people, Jesus said, he goes to the sick.

The Pharisees could not think of any immediate reply to make to this, but they did not like Jesus any the more on that account.

Another time they complained because they said that, according to their rules, there were days when every pious person was supposed to fast, and Jesus and his disciples were not fasting. How did he explain that?

What Jesus replied failed to satisfy them. He said that his disciples could no more fast now than people would fast at a wedding. Fasting was a sign of sorrow; but now that he had come to bring the good news of the Kingdom of God's love it was a time for rejoicing. That did not suit the Pharisees' idea. Their religion was a solemn business. They thought there must be something wrong with anybody as joyous as Jesus was.

But something else happened that offended them still more. On another Sabbath Day Jesus was in the synagogue again; and among the people there was a man with a withered hand. The Pharisees watched Jesus to see what he would do, for one of their stubborn convictions was that nothing could be done on the Sabbath Day that was not necessary. But as soon as Jesus saw the crippled man he said to him, "Come here." Then he turned to the Pharisees, and asked them: "Is it lawful on the Sabbath to do good or to do harm?" They would not answer; and he looked at them with anger.

"Stretch out your hand," Jesus said to the crippled man. The man had thought that he could never again move his hand, but at Jesus' word he did. The hand was restored, as whole now as the other one.

But the little group of Pharisees were more hostile now than ever. They said that Jesus had no business healing on the Sabbath Day. He could have waited until some other time—not *that* time, there in the synagogue. Of course, the crippled man might rejoice that he had been healed, but the Pharisees were not interested in him. What they could not get out of their mind was that Jesus had broken their rules. Now they would do something about it. They went out and began to plot how they could get rid of him.

From that time on Jesus was in danger.

CHAPTER TEN

The Response of the Common People

IT WAS true that Jesus began to be in danger when important people turned against him, but the people in general could not believe ill of him. They followed Jesus everywhere. They saw what he did for the sick and the distressed. They heard him preach about the Kingdom of God. Everything seemed full of hope and gladness wherever he went.

One day when his disciples were gathered about him, he sat on a hillside near the Lake of Galilee and began to tell them about God and about how God could come into their hearts.

"Blessed are the poor in spirit," he said, "for theirs is the Kingdom of heaven.

"Blessed are those who mourn, for they shall be comforted.

"Blessed are the meek, for they shall inherit the earth.

"Blessed are those who hunger and thirst after righteousness, for they shall be satisfied.

"Blessed are the merciful, for they shall obtain mercy.

"Blessed are the pure in heart, for they shall see God.

"Blessed are the peacemakers, for they shall be called sons of God.

"Blessed are those who are persecuted for righteousness' sake, for theirs is the Kingdom of heaven."

As the people listened to Jesus and looked into his face, they had a feeling about God that they had never felt before. It was as though God's love was coming close to *them*. Heretofore, they had supposed that God belonged mostly to the scribes and Pharisees—men who kept all the rules that they said God had given. But Jesus was talking as though God cared just as much for simple people like themselves—people who knew that they were not as good as they ought to be, but who, when they looked at Jesus, wanted to be better. Listen to what he was saying—that the Kingdom of heaven could belong to "the poor in spirit"! That must mean people who had no great opinion of themselves, *their* sort of people. *They* could "hunger and thirst after righteousness." *They* could remember that they were meant to be "children of God."

And this was not all that Jesus said.

"You are the salt of the earth," he went on. "You are the light of the world."

Here was something far beyond what the people had ever dared imagine. The way they themselves lived, and the kind of spirit their humble neighbors saw in them, could be important. If they tried to keep their hearts clean from evil purposes, if they were teachable and patient and kind and true, they could bring their world closer to what God wanted it to be. Like salt, they could keep what was good from being spoiled. Like a city high on a hill, they could be a signal to those who had lost their way. Like a candle, they could give light to those who might have been living in the dark.

That was the wonderful and encouraging part of what Jesus preached. But as they listened to him, they knew that they could not simply drift into the Kingdom of heaven. They had to try, and to try hard, to measure up to what Jesus would expect of those who wanted to learn from him.

He said he had not come to get rid of what the Scriptures had taught concerning God's commandments. He would have their understanding of the commandments go deeper, and change in a man not only the things that he might do, but all his thoughts and innermost desires.

They knew the commandment that they should not kill. Well, that was not enough. They must try also to put all anger and hatred out of their hearts.

They knew the commandment, "You shall not commit adultery." But just because a man might not have actually taken another man's wife did not mean that he had kept the commandment. The commandment also meant that he must keep himself free from lustful thoughts.

They had heard it said that "You shall love your neighbor and hate your enemy." But Jesus said that they must learn to love even those whom they had counted as their enemies, and to pray even for those who persecuted them. "An eye for an eye and a tooth for a tooth" had been another old idea. If anyone did you harm, pay back as much harm—or more—to him. But Jesus said that the goodness of God does not work that way. Do not return evil for evil, but make evil sorry and ashamed by meeting it with kindness. If anyone is violent, meet his violence with gentleness. If anyone forces you to help him, help him more than he has asked. Never mind whether the other man deserves your kindness. Remember God who "makes his sun rise on the evil and on the good, and sends rain on the just and on the unjust."

All the while, if men were trying to live according to God's spirit, they must not make a show of it. Some of the Pharisees, said Jesus, wanted to have everybody know how pious they seemed to be. They liked to say their prayers when they were standing on the corners of the street. If they gave alms to a

beggar, they would do it when they were sure that people were
watching. If they had had a trumpet blown to summon everyone's attention, it would have suited them exactly. But Jesus
said that no one ought to be like that. When you give alms,
let it be so private that even your own left hand can hardly
know what your right hand is doing. And when you pray, let
it be where only God knows and only God is listening.

And how should you pray?

The answer that Jesus gave there in Galilee has come echoing down the years and across the world. For the prayer that he
taught those gathered about him was "The Lord's Prayer."

> Our Father who art in heaven,
> Hallowed be thy name.
> Thy Kingdom come,
> Thy will be done,
> On earth as it is in heaven.
> Give us this day our daily bread;

And forgive us our debts,
As we also have forgiven our debtors;
And lead us not into temptation,
But deliver us from evil.

Sometimes when the Lord's Prayer is repeated, the words are
said differently at one place. Instead of "Forgive us our debts,
as we also have forgiven our debtors," those who are praying
may say, "Forgive us our trespasses, as we forgive those who
trespass against us." Either way is true to what Jesus taught;
and finally to the whole prayer are added the thankful words:
"For thine is the kingdom, and the power, and the glory, for
ever and ever. Amen."

That day on the hillside in Galilee, when Jesus taught the
people in what is remembered as "The Sermon on the Mount,"
he spoke to them especially of the love of God which they could
trust for all their needs. "Do not be anxious," he said. They
were not to worry all the time about what they could have to
eat and what they could wear. Look at the birds singing in
hedgerows, and the golden lilies growing in the fields. God
gave the birds their food, and he made the lilies more beautiful than the dress of kings. And God cares still more for his
human children. They were not to go about borrowing
trouble, then, but to live each day faithfully and trust God
for the days to come.

All this and much more Jesus said to the people who gathered around him. As he looked at them he knew that different
sorts of men and women were in that throng. Some were what
their neighbors called "well-off"; a few might even be rich,
imagining they already possessed everything that mattered.
But all the same their lives could be starved and empty unless
God came into their hearts.

On the other hand, many who were there were poor. Jesus
loved them all the more because he understood what they had
to go through when times were hard. But even when they were

poor, they could know so much of the goodness of God that they would feel richer than the rich. Your Father knows all the everyday things you need, he said. So let your thoughts go on to what is greater. "Seek his Kingdom and his righteousness, and all these things shall be yours as well."

So Jesus spoke, and the people listened. And when he finished they knew that they had not just been listening to words. They had begun to understand that the only way by which whatever they lived and worked for could stand up was by building it upon what Jesus taught. He asked them if they remembered what happened to different sorts of houses when a great storm came. Here was one house that looked well enough, but had for its foundations nothing but sand. When winds blew and rain fell so heavily that floods rolled along the ground, the foundations of that house were washed away, and the whole house collapsed. But here was another house built upon a rock, and no storms or floods could move it.

No wonder it was said of Jesus then that "The crowds were astonished at his teaching, for he taught them as one who had authority, and not as the scribes."

CHAPTER ELEVEN

What the Disciples Began to Learn

WHERE did Jesus get his authority? Those who did not want to listen to him complained that he had no right to speak. The scribes and Pharisees in Galilee said that; and so did others who came all the way from Jerusalem, the capital, to find out what Jesus was doing. Jesus, they said, did not teach what was proper. He did not keep the thousand and one rules which they, the Pharisees and scribes, had added to the law of Moses. *They* were the important leaders of the Jewish Church. *They* had not given him any commission to teach the people, or to heal the sick. And if they had not given him such commission, they did not believe that God had done so either.

But the disciples knew where Jesus' authority came from. They saw him go out into the hills for hours and hours to be alone to think and to pray. Once, when they looked for him, they found that he had gone in the night, long before the daybreak. When he returned and they saw his face, they knew that the light of God was in his eyes.

Jesus began now to choose other men to be among his closest friends and disciples. The four already with him were Peter and Andrew, and James and John. One day as he went through a town he saw a man named Matthew who was sitting at a toll-booth where he collected taxes. Now anyone who was a tax collector was hated and despised, for the taxes were for the Roman empire, or else for Herod, the ruler whom the Romans had given power in Galilee in the name of Rome. It seemed to the people of Israel, therefore, that tax collectors were not much better than traitors, for they appeared to have sold out their Jewish loyalty for the sake of Roman money. Also, tax collectors were often dishonest, making the people pay more taxes than they really owed. It was natural, therefore, to think that tax-collector Matthew would be the last man whom Jesus would choose for a disciple.

But, to the crowd's astonishment, Jesus stopped in front of Matthew. "Come with me," he said. Matthew himself was as astonished as all the rest. Yet he got straight up and came fumbling out of his office to go with Jesus. And that was the last he had to do with tax collecting. The fact was that Matthew was a different sort of man from what people supposed. They judged him by the business he was in, and by the look of things. But Jesus had a way of seeing through the outside of a man, clear to what he was in his own heart. He knew that Matthew wanted something better than he had ever known—and that when he saw that something in Jesus, he would leave his tax collecting and everything else, to follow.

Matthew's friends probably had no better reputation than Matthew himself had had. Jesus was not going to let himself associate with such as these, Matthew must have thought. Certainly the Pharisees would have been horrified at such a possibility. But people like Matthew's friends were exactly the sort that Jesus was always reaching out for. Jesus said he had come to seek "the lost sheep of the house of Israel"—that is to say, the people who had gone wandering off into sinful ways because they were headstrong, or because no one had ever been to them like a shepherd who cared what happened to them. So Jesus let Matthew invite his friends to dinner and he sat in the midst of them. And men who had never thought

much about the love of God knew then what it was as they
looked at Jesus.

As Jesus called Matthew, so also he called some other men
to be his disciples. These were their names: Philip, Bartholo-
mew, Thomas, James (another James, whose father was
Alphaeus, and so was of a different family from James, the
son of Zebedee, who had followed Jesus that first day from the
fishing boat on the Lake of Galilee), Thaddeus, Simon, and
Judas Iscariot. Simon was sometimes called the Zealot, which
meant that he was one of the group of Jewish patriots who
hated the Roman rule and were forever hoping that a great
leader would come to rally an army round him and set the
people free. It may be that he thought at first that Jesus would
be that kind of leader; and so, perhaps in a darker and more
secret way, did Judas.

Even the closest of the disciples could not understand Jesus
fully. His thoughts were always greater than their thoughts.
The disciples, like all other human beings, could have ideas
that were selfish and narrow. Sometimes they wondered about
honors which might come to them because they belonged to
Jesus. More often they were thinking of special blessings
which might come only to the people of Israel, and not to their
enemies. In the old days there had been the glorious kingdom
of David and Solomon. Why not another and greater kingdom,
with its capital in Jerusalem, instead of the empire that was
held together by the armies of Rome?

But Jesus was looking forward to something far more wonderful. He was not concerned with earthly empires created by
wars and killing which stand for a little while and then are
overthrown by the hatred of those they have subdued. He
had come to call men into the Kingdom of God, which could
be as wide as the world. If once the hearts of men could be

ruled by the love of God, then all peoples could live in a
brotherhood of gladness and of peace.

Meanwhile the disciples, as they followed Jesus, could begin
to learn what life in the Kingdom of God could mean. They
saw him always forgetting about himself because he was so
quick to see the needs of others. They saw how the love of
God shone through Jesus to make people ashamed of their sins
and to encourage them when they wanted to be better. Com-
pared to the joy and power that he had, and that he gave to
those around him, what else could possibly be worth wanting?

So they came to understand, in their own ways, what Jesus
said when he talked about the Kingdom of God—or the Kingdom of heaven, as he sometimes called it. He said that it was
like a grain of mustard seed, a seed so small that one could
hardly see it, but which, when planted, grew up into a bush
so tall that the birds made nests in its branches. And he said
also that it was like the tiny measure of yeast which a woman
kneaded into the bowl of meal—to spread through the whole
of it, and make it into bread.

Yes, that was just the way it had been with them. At first,
what they knew about God had looked so small that they could
hardly imagine it would grow and spread, like the seed and
like the yeast. But it did. Their whole life was different, their
whole world seemed different, because of the Spirit of God
that was at work.

And, another day, they knew what Jesus meant when he
described the Kingdom of God in one of his parables that no
one could forget. (To teach by parables was a favorite way of
Jesus, for a parable means making a great truth plain by showing that it is like some simple thing which everyone understands.) The Kingdom of God, he said, is like a treasure hidden in a field. To the people who listened to him that day,
those words must have had an exciting sound. For there *had*

been treasures hidden in the fields of Palestine, and some of them might be still there. The plain of Esdraelon at the foot of the hills had been a battleground century after century, for longer than they could remember. Armies from the seacoast and the desert, from the south and from the east, had moved across it on their way to war and plunder. There the Philistines had come against the army of Saul. There the terrible chariots of the Assyrians had rolled; and Egyptians and Babylonians had met in deadly conflict. When the people living in the little villages knew that another war had broken out and that another enemy might be ravaging the land, they would go out and hide whatever they had that was most valuable in the ground. Then those same people might be killed, or carried off as captives, and so they would never come back to dig up what they had buried. Long years afterward, someone ploughing a field might suddenly come upon the hidden treasures, to his astonishment and joy.

Such also could be the excitement of the man who found in his heart the treasure of a new life when he had begun to search for the Kingdom of God.

But Jesus knew that not everyone would listen to what he taught. Some people were satisfied to stay the way they were. They were not ready to have him teach them anything, because then they would have to change old ideas which they did not choose to change.

CHAPTER TWELVE

Jesus Goes
Back to Nazareth

ONE DAY Jesus went back to Nazareth, his own home town. It was the Sabbath, and so he went to church, as he always did. After the service in the synagogue had begun, the one who was leading it asked Jesus to read from the Scriptures. So Jesus read from the Book of the prophet Isaiah.

"The Spirit of the Lord is upon me,
because he has anointed me to preach good news to the poor.
He has sent me to proclaim release to the captives,
and recovering of sight to the blind,
to set at liberty those who are oppressed,
to proclaim the acceptable year of the Lord."

When he had finished reading, he said to the congregation, "Today this scripture has been fulfilled." What Isaiah had prophesied about the preaching of the good news from God had come true.

Some of the people liked what they heard, and others were not too sure. They looked at Jesus and remembered how they had seen him and known him through the years when he was living there in Nazareth. Now he had come back again and was being welcomed as someone important. "Isn't this Joseph's son?" some of them asked. "His mother and the others of the family are still here, people like the rest of us. How, then," they wanted to know, "did he come to have authority?"

The report was that he had been doing great things in Capernaum and in other towns—healing people, working miracles. But how did they know this was really true? And, if it *were* true, let Jesus show here and now what he could do in his home town.

Jesus could see what was going on in their thoughts and hear what was being whispered. It was a sad thing that these neighbors in Nazareth, who, most of all, should have welcomed him when he came with the message of the love of God, should be only curious and suspicious.

He said to them: "Doubtless you will quote this proverb to me: 'Physician, heal yourself.' We have heard what you did in Capernaum. Now let us see what you can do in your own country." In other words, they were saying, "It is all very well for you to have a reputation somewhere else. But don't expect us to be excited unless you do something exciting here."

Jesus looked at them and he knew that they did not really

want a message from God—anyhow, not unless it came in a way that suited them. They were not going to admit that he could come back here to the synagogue in Nazareth and tell them something they did not know already. Instead of being eager for the power of God which they might have seen at work in him, they were only jealous.

When people will not listen and will not learn, they can be deaf to everything that God would say to them. Then all that God would have given them must pass them by, to be received perhaps by someone else. That is the way it had often been, said Jesus. In his own country, a prophet may have no honor. Jesus also said to the congregation that they could open the Scriptures and read how it was in the days of the great Elijah. Who was it that turned to the prophet then in faith and was helped and blessed? Not anyone in Israel, but an outsider, a poor woman in the city of Sidon. And in the days of Elisha, who was it that was healed of leprosy? Not any one of the many lepers in Israel, but Naaman the Syrian. So it would be again. The mighty works that Jesus might have wrought in Nazareth could not be done, because the men and women there in Nazareth had no faith.

When the people heard this, they were filled with anger. So they were not to see anything special after all! Jesus, who was said to have worked miracles in other places, was not going to work any miracles for them. Moreover, Jesus had talked as though God's salvation might be just as likely to come to outside people as to themselves, who had been attending the synagogue all their life. How could they be expected to stand that? So they rose up furiously against Jesus. They wanted to push him off the edge of the hill above the town. But before the look in his eyes they fell back, and he passed straight through the crowd who did not quite dare to lay hands upon him, and went on his way. So far as the Gospels tell, Jesus did not come back to Nazareth again.

There was another town which also missed its chance, as
Nazareth had done, though in a different way. Once Jesus,
with his disciples, was passing through the district of Samaria.
At the end of the day, as it began to grow dark, they came to
a Samaritan village, and Jesus sent James and John ahead to
ask whether he and the disciples could stay there that night.
But there existed an old hatred between the Samaritans and
the Jewish people in general: and when the Samaritan villagers
learned that these men on the road came from Galilee, they
said they would have nothing to do with any of them. Of
course they did not know who Jesus was, but if they had been
more generous they might have had him in their village; sick
people might have been made well, and troubled people comforted, and little children blessed. Now they would never
know him, and never have the blessing he would have brought.
James and John were indignant. They said they wished God
would strike a village like that with lightning and wipe it
from the face of the earth. But Jesus rebuked them. They had
no understanding, he said, of what their spirit ought to be.
Hadn't they learned that he had come not to destroy men's
lives, but to save them?

To save: that was what he was always reaching out to do. No
matter who men were, if they would respond to Jesus, there
was no limit to his patience and his love.

CHAPTER THIRTEEN

The Outreaching Mercy

THE GOSPEL of John tells of another time when Jesus passed
through Samaria. He stopped by an ancient well which was
said to have been the well where hundreds and hundreds of
years before Jacob had watered his flocks. While Jesus was
alone there, a Samaritan woman came to the well to draw
water. When Jesus asked her for a drink of the water she was
drawing, the woman was surprised. How did he happen to ask
that?—she wanted to know. He belonged to the Jewish people,
and she was a Samaritan; and there were not supposed to be
any dealings between them.

Jesus gave her a surprising answer. He said that, yes, he had
asked her for some of the water that had to be drawn up from
the well. But if she should ask him, he could give her living
water—water that flowed forever of its own accord.

What was he talking about?—the woman wondered. Who
was he, anyway? "You have nothing to draw water with, and
this well is deep. Where are you going to find any 'living
water'? Are you greater than our father Jacob who gave us this
well, and used it for himself and his sons and all his cattle?"

Jesus answered her once more. People who drank of this well
would be thirsty again. "But whoever drinks of the water that
I shall give him will never thirst," he said; "the water that I
shall give him will become a spring of water welling up to
eternal life."

I wish this man would give me a spring of water like that,

the woman thought. Then I would not have to be coming here all the time to draw water up.

She supposed Jesus was talking of her kind of water, only made easier to get. She did not understand yet that he was speaking of another kind of water—the water that he could give to those whose souls were thirsty for God, even though they did not know it.

Jesus looked at her and pitied her, for he saw that she was unhappy. She had had a hard life, and there were things about it of which she was ashamed. He told her to go and call her husband. She admitted that she had no husband. It seemed to her that Jesus was beginning to know all about her, and it made her uneasy.

"Our fathers worshiped on this mountain," she said; "and you say that in Jerusalem is the place where men ought to worship." Perhaps she could keep Jesus from getting too close to her life by starting an argument.

But Jesus knew that deep down she wanted something better than an argument. Old-time disputes did not matter. What did matter was that God should come into her own life to make it better. So he told her about God, and about how God's Spirit could come close to her. And the woman went away and told all the people in her Samaritan town that this man from Galilee who had spoken to her at the well knew her better than she knew herself.

Wherever Jesus went, he was sure to be quick to see somebody who needed help.

One day he was with the disciples on the Lake of Galilee. They crossed over in their boat to the other side of the lake, to the district of Gadara. They had hardly stepped ashore when a terrible-looking creature came dashing toward them, a man who was insane. He had no home of his own; he hid out among the tombs in a graveyard. The people in the nearby town

Jesus summons Matthew the tax collector to follow him.

"Little girl, I say to you, arise."

were afraid of him, and they had tried to chain him up. But he had broken his chains and was loose.

As he ran toward Jesus, he screamed out that Jesus had nothing to do with him. Jesus should let him alone. Then suddenly, in some wild burst of understanding, he seemed to recognize in the same moment that there was something wonderful about Jesus. He threw himself down at Jesus' feet, as though to worship him.

Then Jesus turned his great eyes upon the wild face that looked up to him. The power of a great pity was in Jesus' voice. Here in front of him was this man who was like two men, with some dreadful evil spirit in him which had taken the place of his real self.

"Come out of him!" said Jesus.

The man gave a great cry, shuddered, and then was quiet. The disciples held their breath. Yes, it was true! This lunatic was healed.

On the open ground nearby there was a herd of pigs. With all the noise of the wild man's screaming they were thrown into a panic, and they ran. There was a steep place that dropped down sharply to the lake, and some of the herd plunged over it and were drowned.

When the people of the neighborhood heard the excitement they came out to see what was happening. To their amazement, they saw the man who had been crazy completely changed, and in his right mind. But the men who owned the pigs discovered something else. Something had happened to their pigs that was more important to them than what had happened to the man. Part of their herd was dead. That made them so annoyed that the great thing Jesus had done did not matter. Healing or no healing, they did not want Jesus around. They told him that they would rather that he left their country.

When Jesus and the disciples were ready to go back across the lake, the man who had been cured begged to go with them. But Jesus told him to stay in his own land, and go to those who used to be his friends and tell them what the power of God had done for him.

CHAPTER FOURTEEN

The Power of God in Jesus

AFTER Jesus had returned to the side of the lake where Capernaum was, the people flocked around him, as they always did. And among them came one of the chief men of the synagogue, named Jairus, who bowed down at Jesus' feet to beseech him. "My little daughter," he cried, "my little daughter! She is at the point of death. Come and lay your hands on her, so that she may be made well, and live!"

So Jesus started out at once toward Jairus' house. But even before he could get there something beautiful happened. In the crowd that followed there was a woman who had been sick a long time. She had been to many physicians, and had paid them nearly everything she had, but none of them had done her any good. Instead of getting better, she had grown worse. But when she looked at Jesus, she believed that he could do more for her than all the doctors. "If I could just touch his cloak," she said, "I would be healed."

Timidly she pressed through the other people until she came close enough to Jesus to reach out and touch him. He stopped and turned around. "Who was it that touched me?" he asked.

The disciples were surprised at his asking such a question. Here were the people crowding and jostling all around. Any number of them might have touched him. What did he mean by asking *who* it was that touched him?

But Jesus knew that there had been a touch that was different—not just accidental, and not cautious—but full of great longing and hope. In response to that, he had felt the power going out of himself to meet somebody's urgent need.

Trembling, the woman admitted that she was the one who had reached out to him. And she knelt down at his feet and told him all her distress, and how she had hoped that he would do what no one else had been able to do for her.

"Daughter, your faith has made you well," he said. "Go in peace, and be healed of your disease."

That was on the road to Jairus' house. Just at that moment, a messenger met them and said to Jairus, "Your daughter is dead." There was no longer any use in asking Jesus to come.

But Jesus said to Jairus, "Do not be afraid. Only believe."

Then he told all the crowd to stand back and stay where they were. He took only Peter and James and John with him, and they went into Jairus' house. All the people there were weeping and wailing, and the place was in a tumult.

"Why do you make all this lamentation?" Jesus asked. "The child is not dead but sleeping."

They looked at him scornfully. Some of them even laughed. How could he stand there and tell them the child was not dead?

But Jesus put all of them outside, took Jairus and the child's mother and his three disciples and went into the room where the little girl was lying. *"Talitha cumi,"* he said, which meant, "Little girl, I say to you arise."

Immediately she did so, and when Jesus held out his hands she walked to him. Then he told them to give her something to eat.

The disciples who were with Jesus all the time marvelled more and more at how wonderful he was. Of course they had been taught about God and they believed in God; but no one had ever made them know the greatness of God, and the nearness of God, as Jesus did.

Seeing Jesus' compassion for the poor and the sick and

the distressed, they understood that God was not someone far-off and unconcerned, but that he was *there* in the love that was in Jesus. And when they saw what Jesus did, they began to think that there was nothing that could not happen when the power of God worked through him.

One evening they were out on the lake in one of the fishing boats which Peter and Andrew and some of the others knew so well. The Lake of Galilee can be calm and still. But there are hills around it, the Jordan River cuts a deep valley to the south, and to the north rises the mighty snow-crowned mountain peak of Hermon, so that the winds change suddenly and squalls may break with unexpected danger. Some eight miles wide and thirteen miles from end to end, the lake is not a very big one, as great lakes go, but it is wide enough and long enough for storms to whip its water into racing waves which can swamp a boat.

This time the disciples were caught far out from shore as black clouds boiled up, and in the gathering darkness the wind mounted to a gale that churned the lake to blinding foam and spray. Waves beat into the boat, and it began to fill so fast that even these men, so long accustomed to managing boats, were terrified lest it should sink. Jesus was with them, but he had put his head on a cushion in the stern of the boat, and he was asleep. The disciples woke him. "Master, master!" they cried through the screaming of the wind, "don't you care that we are about to perish?"

Jesus opened his eyes and looked first at the storm and then at his disciples. Why were they in such a panic? They could ride this storm out. "Peace, be still!" he said to the mounting waves. And to the astonishment of his companions, the wind went down as suddenly as it had come, the waves flattened, and presently they were on their way to shore.

After a time Jesus decided that these men who had been

with him so long could do more than learn; they could teach also. They should begin to go out now and bring to other people the good news of what God would do for them. So Jesus sent them two by two. They were to stop wherever men would listen to them and stay as long as they were welcomed. They were to preach repentance, and they were to help everybody that they could.

When they came back to Jesus, they were full of glad excitement. They had been given power to do what they had hardly believed they could do. They said that in the name of God, and in the way they had learned from Jesus, they had been able to get the evil spirits out of some of the people they had preached to, and to lay their hands on sick people and to make them well.

Then Jesus took them out with him into a lonely place. They needed to come close to God in thankfulness and prayer. There he would hear from them all they had to tell.

But it was not easy to get away from the crowd. People had seen the disciples launch the boat that was to take them with Jesus across the lake; but they went on foot around the shore, and when the boat landed a crowd was already there.

The disciples might have thought that Jesus would be annoyed. He had come away from the Capernaum shore so that for a little while he might have only the disciples with him, for in the recent days there had been so many people coming and going that he had had no leisure even to eat. But Jesus, as always, could forget such things when he saw those who needed what he could give. As it is written in the Gospel of Mark, he looked at the throng "and he had compassion on them, because they were like sheep without a shepherd; and he began to teach them many things."

The day went by, and it grew late. The disciples came to Jesus and they said to him that this place where they were was a long way from home. It was nearly night and these people were hungry. Hadn't he better send them away to see if they could find some village where they could buy food?

"Give them something to eat," Jesus answered.

But how on earth, they wondered, could they do that? How could they get together enough to feed all these people? Philip calculated how much it would cost to buy enough bread for all of them—even if each were to have only a little. It would be a lot of money, and they did not have it.

Then Jesus asked what food there was already that they knew of.

Andrew, Peter's brother, said "There is a lad here who has five barley loaves and two fish; but what are they among so many?"

Jesus said to have the people sit down. Then he took the loaves and gave thanks, and broke the bread to be handed out among the people. He did the same with the fish. Somehow, in a way the disciples could not understand, the bread and the fish that Jesus had blessed were enough. All the people's hunger was satisfied, and there was even food left over. Now, more than ever, the disciples knew that when they had Jesus, there was no need that could not be met.

But men's memories can be short. One day not long afterwards, Jesus and his disciples went on a journey, and, on arriving at their journey's end they discovered that the food they had meant to bring along had been left behind. Then there was great concern and argument as to how they would make out. But Jesus reminded them of what had happened when they thought that five loaves and two fish were all they had with which to feed the multitude. What God felt they needed would be supplied. Furthermore, they needed to learn that the important matter was not whether at any particular moment they had all that they had expected to have to eat.

What *was* important was that their minds should be fed by the thought of God and their hearts by the love of God—this would give them, Jesus said, "not the food that perishes, but the food that endures to eternal life."

CHAPTER FIFTEEN

To Seek and Save the Lost

IT WAS said of Jesus that "the common people heard him gladly." They felt that he cared about them all. There was no one in need or in trouble for whom he did not have compassion. He treated the most ordinary person—even the person for whom others had no use—as important in the sight of God.

Some of the Pharisees and scribes were not like that. They were proud and separate. They had their own harsh ideas of what it meant to be religious; and little by little their religion had become mostly a matter of show rather than of actual spirit. Everything had to be done according to the correct tradition. There was a pattern in clothes which was supposed to be pious. There were proper customs to be followed all day long, concerning what they could do and ought not to do, what they ate and how and when they fasted, and those with whom they could or could not associate. They said that all these rules of theirs were part of the law of God that had come down from Moses, and that everybody's first duty was to obey them. But unfortunately, the holier they appeared on the surface, the more self-satisfied they grew, until their hearts were hard. They despised the same common people whom Jesus pitied. And the people, for their part, began to doubt whether these scribes and Pharisees could be as religious as they looked. Would God be as hard on ordinary people as these teachers were? If so, then most of them would be left out of God's Kingdom.

But then they looked at Jesus, and it was no wonder that they heard him gladly. Not only did he bring them a new gospel; he put it in language they could understand.

One day a crowd, in which were tax collectors and other men of shady reputation, gathered round him. The Pharisees and scribes complained: "This man receives sinners and eats with them."

Jesus answered with three parables:

He said first: "What man of you, having a hundred sheep, if he has lost one of them, does not leave the ninety-nine in the wilderness, and go after the one which is lost, until he finds it? And when he has found it, he lays it on his shoulders, rejoicing. And when he comes home, he calls together his friends and his neighbors, saying to them, 'Rejoice with me, for I have found my sheep which was lost.' Even so, I tell you, there will be more joy in heaven over one sinner who repents than over ninety-nine righteous persons who need no repentance."

All the men who day by day saw the sheep on the Galilean hills and who knew the ways of shepherds could understand that. Those in whose poor little homes every small possession was precious, knew instantly how real was Jesus' next parable.

"What woman, having ten silver coins," said Jesus, "and losing one coin, does not light a lamp and sweep the house and seek diligently until she finds it? And when she has found it, she calls together her friends and neighbors, saying, 'Rejoice with me, for I have found the coin which had lost.' Even so,

I tell you, there is joy before the angels of God over one sinner who repents."

Then he told them a third parable, which is usually spoken of as "The Parable of the Prodigal Son." But as a matter of fact, that word "prodigal" is not in the parable anywhere. It is a story about two sons, and their father, and especially about one of the sons, who—like most people who go wrong—did not start out deliberately to be wicked. He was headstrong and know-it-all, and so in his foolishness got into disastrous trouble.

This son was one of the sort of young people who grow restless at home and think they must go out and see life on their own. So, as Jesus told of him, he asked his father to give him in advance the part of the family inheritance that was to belong to him later on. And his father did so.

Then the son went off and began to spend what he had. As long as he had money to throw about in loose living, there were many who pretended to be his friends. But after a while, when his money was gone, and he had nothing left with which to buy even food, nobody bothered about him or gave him so much as something to eat. He had to hire himself out to take care of hogs, and he fed himself from the scraps.

Then, in Jesus' words, "he came to himself." He began to understand what he ought to have been doing all along as his father's decent son. He remembered that in his father's house even the servants had plenty to eat, and yet here was he, perishing with hunger. "I will arise and go to my father," he said, "and I will say to him, Father, I have sinned against heaven and before you. I am no longer worthy to be called your son; treat me as one of your hired servants."

So he started home. But before he had reached there his father saw him in the distance, and ran to meet him, and took him in his arms and kissed him.

"I have sinned!" the boy said. "I am no longer worthy to be called your son."

But the father told his servants to bring the best clothes they could find and put them on his son, and to put a ring on his hand. And they were to kill a calf that had been fattened to make a special feast. "For this my son," he said, "was dead and is alive again! He was lost, and is found."

This part of the parable was for the sake of those who knew that they were sinners, and needed to believe that, even so, God cared for them—as the father in the story yearned for the son who had gone astray. Then Jesus added another part to the parable, directing it at some of the scribes and Pharisees who were more concerned with getting credit for their own righteousness than they were in reaching out in mercy to those who had gone wrong.

When the younger son came back, the parable continued, the elder son was in the field. "And as he came and drew near to the house, he heard music and dancing. And he called one of the servants and asked what this meant. And he said to him, 'Your brother has come, and your father has killed the fatted calf, because he has received him safe and sound.' But he was angry and refused to go in. His father came out and entreated him, but he answered his father, 'Lo, these many years I have served you, and I never disobeyed your command; yet you never gave me a kid, that I might make merry with my friends. But when this son of yours came, who has devoured your living with harlots, you killed for him the fatted calf!' "

Then the father answered: "Son, you are always with me, and all that is mine is yours. It was fitting to make merry and be glad, for this your brother was dead, and is alive; he was lost, and is found."

The pity was that so many of those who were supposed to

be the most religious people did not want to feel the way the
parable might have made them feel. Jealous, and proud of
their own piety, they were not going to associate with sinners
if they could help it. It annoyed them to be told that they were
supposed to be concerned about people who had been dis-
reputable.

One day Jesus was invited to dinner by a Pharisee named
Simon. While they were at dinner, there stole into the house
a woman who was a sinner. Everybody knew her reputation,
but none of those who had taken their pleasure with her knew
what was in her heart. Somewhere she had seen Jesus and had
heard him; and suddenly, like the younger son in the parable,
she came to herself—to her real self, ashamed of the life she
had been living, penitent, and passionate now with a new kind
of love which was altogether pure. Jesus had changed her, and
she must somehow show her gratitude and devotion. So, before
any of the servants could stop her, she appeared in the banquet room, close to where Jesus was. She had brought with
her a jar of very precious ointment. She broke the jar, and
poured the ointment on Jesus' feet, so that the whole room was
filled with fragrance. The tears poured down from her eyes,
and she wiped them away with her beautiful long hair.

Simon, the host, was scandalized. No such person as this was
ever supposed to be admitted into his house; and what sort of
person was Jesus if he let this woman touch him? That is what
he was thinking, and Jesus could read it in his face.

"Simon," said Jesus, "I have something to say to you."

"What is it?" said Simon.

"There was a certain creditor," Jesus said, "who had two
debtors. One of them owed him ten times as much as the
other. When they could not pay, he forgave them both. Now
which of them will love him more?"

Simon answered, "The one, I suppose, to whom he forgave more."

Jesus said to him, "You have judged rightly."

Then, turning toward the woman, he said to Simon, "Do you

see this woman? I entered your house. You gave me no water for my feet, but she has wet my feet with her tears and wiped them with her hair. You gave me no kiss, but from the time I came in she has not ceased to kiss my feet. You did not anoint my head with oil, but she has anointed my feet with ointment. Therefore, I tell you, her sins which are many, are forgiven, for she loved much."

And he said to her, "Your sins are forgiven. Your faith has saved you; go in peace."

There was another woman also who was protected by Jesus' understanding mercy. In the Gospel of John is the account of what happened to her. She was married, but she had been false to her husband, and had gone off sinfully with another man. Both of them had been caught, and some of the Pharisees heard of it. But it was only the woman whom the Pharisees were concerned to punish. They brought her, trembling and alone, to Jesus. They said that Moses had commanded in the law that a woman like her should be stoned to death. What did Jesus have to say to that?

He looked at those men, who were so hard and so self-righteous, and he knew that though they looked so pious there were sinful passions in their hearts. He stooped down and began to write something with his finger in the dust. They could not see what he was writing, but they were to learn soon enough what his word for them would be. Jesus stood up and looked them in the face. "Let him who is without sin among you be the first to throw a stone at her," he said.

Once more he stooped down and wrote with his finger in the dust; and before his eyes could be on them again, the Pharisees began to move off one by one. When Jesus looked up, the last of them was gone.

He turned to the woman. "Where are they now?" he asked. "Has no one condemned you?" "No one, Lord," she answered. And Jesus said, "Neither do I condemn you. Go, and do not sin again."

In a world that had in it so many twisted thoughts and so much evil, Jesus could see, as no other could, where God's righteousness and God's mercy pointed. So he could say of himself, "I am the light of the world."

CHAPTER SIXTEEN

The Blind See
and the Sick Are Healed

THAT DAY in the house of Simon the Pharisee was only one of the many times when Jesus showed his compassion for someone whom others had condemned.

According to the Gospel of John, he went up to Jerusalem to one of the great festivals, and saw there a man who had been born blind. The disciples asked him why it was that this man should be so afflicted. Was it because his parents had committed some sin? Or was it because God was punishing the man himself?

No, neither one was true, said Jesus. But because of this man's blindness, they would have a chance now to see the power of the love of God.

Jesus called the blind man to him. He made clay and put it on the blind man's eyes. Then he said to him, "Go to the pool of Siloam and wash."

Obediently the blind man groped his way to the pool. He washed his eyes as Jesus had told him to do; and to his amazement, he could see.

All the people who had known him were excited.

"Isn't this the man who used to sit and beg?" they asked one another.

"Yes, it is," said some. Others said they were not sure.

Maybe he was someone else, who only looked like the blind beggar.

But the beggar himself answered, "I am the man."

Some of the Pharisees heard what had happened, and had the man brought before them. It was on the Sabbath Day that he had been healed, and the Pharisees were angered because of that.

How was it, they wanted to know, that he had got his sight? He was to tell them exactly everything about it.

"He put clay on my eyes, and I washed, and I could see," the man said. He told the story so clearly that it was hard for anyone to deny what had happened; but they were not going to believe him unless they had to.

They sent for the man's parents. "Is this your son?" they demanded. Yes, he was. "You say he was born blind?" Yes, they answered, that was so. Well, then, let them explain how it was that now he could see.

The parents were afraid of these important leaders of the church. They said yes, this *was* their son, and he had been born blind, but they didn't know a thing about how he had suddenly got his sight, or who had cured him—or anything. Please not to ask them. Let them go, and call their son back, and have him answer for himself.

So they did call him back. They knew now that it was Jesus who had healed him, and healed him on the Sabbath Day. So here was this troublesome disturber whom they had already heard about as having come from Nazareth, breaking the Sabbath law and upsetting things again!

"Give God the praise," they said to the man who had been blind. "As for this man who healed you, we know that he is a sinner."

But the former blind man said he didn't know about that. All he knew was that he had been blind, and now he could see.

The Pharisees who were examining him would not let him

alone. They were not going to admit that Jesus had done anything as wonderful as this man said. And if he *had* done it,
they were just as annoyed anyway because all this had happened on a Sabbath Day.

So the Pharisees began to badger the man with more cross-
examination. They wanted to know exactly what it was that
Jesus did, and they way he did it. *How* did he open your
eyes?" they demanded.

The man had been only a poor blind beggar, but when the
Pharisees kept insisting, he was not afraid to answer back. "I
told you already," he said, "and you would not listen. Why do
you want to hear it all again? Do you want to become his disciples?"

The Pharisees took that question for an insult, and they spat
out their indignant answer. "You are his disciple," they said,
"but we are disciples of Moses. We know that God has spoken
to Moses, but as for this man, we do not know where he comes
from."

But the man who had been blind was not to be put to
silence. He had the courage to keep on standing up for what
he knew to be the truth.

"Why, this is a queer thing," he said. "You do not know
where he comes from, and yet he opened my eyes. We know
that God does not listen to sinners, but if any one is a wor-
shiper of God and does his will, God listens to him. Never
since the world began has it been heard that any one has
opened the eyes of a man born blind. If this man were not
from God, he could not do anything."

"You were born in utter sin!" cried the Pharisees scornfully.
"Do you think you can teach us?" And they drove the man out.

Now Jesus heard of what the Pharisees had done, and he
looked for the man and found him. "Do you believe in the
Son of man?" asked Jesus. The man who had been blind did
not know much about names, but there was one thing he did

know. He believed in Jesus. He would stand up to that, any-where and everywhere.

Then Jesus, thinking of the difference between this man and the supposedly learned people who ought to have been quicker than he to recognize the words of God, said, "For judgment I came into this world, that those who do not see may see, and that those who see may become blind."

Some of the Pharisees heard about this, and they came to Jesus and asked him, "Are you saying, then, that we are blind?"

And Jesus answered, "If you were blind, you would have no guilt; but now that you say 'We see,' your guilt remains."

As Jesus went on his way, whether in Galilee or elsewhere, there was the same difference in people that there had been between the blind man and the Pharisees. There were some who could see that in Jesus something beautiful and saving had come near; and there were others who could not see this because they did not like some of the things which Jesus had said and done.

One day a Roman centurion came to Jesus. In general, the Romans had contempt for the people of Israel, and it might have been supposed that a commander of Roman soldiers especially would not have turned for help to anyone not a Roman. But the Roman's servant was sick, and he was sorry for him. The centurion knew of Jesus; and as a man of author-ity himself, he recognized authority when he saw it. So when he had come to Jesus and told him of his sick servant, he said he was sure that Jesus could make the man well again. It was not necessary, he said, that Jesus even come to his house. "Only say the word, and my servant will be healed."

Jesus said that not even in Israel had he found a faith like that. And the centurion's faith should have its answer. "Go," said Jesus, "it shall be done for you as you have believed." And from that moment the servant was well.

On another day Jesus had gone out of Galilee to the sea-coast region near the cities of Tyre and Sidon. A woman there had a little daughter who was said to be "possessed by an unclean spirit"—which meant that she was out of her mind. The woman came to Jesus and begged him to heal her child.

It seemed at first as though Jesus were putting her off. He was watching perhaps to see how deep her need might be, and how genuine her faith. Why, he asked, did she suppose he would be interested in foreign people? Didn't she know—or think she knew—that he had come for the sake of the children of Israel, and only for them? Why should the children's bread be given to the dogs?

The woman knew well enough that in the mixed-up world of Galilee and the regions round it there were peoples who despised each other. But she looked at Jesus' face, and she knew how different he was from the words with which he had been testing her. She could see the smile that played about his mouth, and the great compassion in his eyes. "Yes, Lord," she said, "I know. But can't even the dogs under the table have the children's crumbs?"

So she had understood! She had known—in spite of what anyone might have told her—that Jesus would be concerned for her, no matter if she was of another race. Jesus answered her plea. Go home, he told her, and she would find her little daughter healed.

Who could tell which men and women would respond to the gospel of God, and which would not. What happens in the hearts of people, Jesus said, is like what may happen in the ground when a sower goes out in the springtime to scatter seed in the ploughed field. Some of that seed may fall where someone has walked across the ground and trodden a hard path, so that the seed lies on the surface and birds fly down and carry it away. Some of the seed falls where the ground is rocky. The grain will begin to grow, but it has no deep root, and when the hot sun comes it will be scorched. And some seed falls among weeds which will spring up and choke it. But there will also be the good ground, open and soft and ready for the sowing; and the grain falling there will grow and multiply thirty times, sixty times, a hundred times.

And so it is with the seed of the new life that can come from God.

CHAPTER SEVENTEEN

The Shadow of
Approaching Danger

THE CROWDS continued to flock around Jesus, and it seemed that his hold upon the people grew greater every day. But actually there were increasing signs of something different happening. Since the time when he first came back to Galilee after the baptism at the Jordan River, little knots of Pharisees and scribes had been whispering against him. Now other forces were added to theirs. Danger was threatening, like storm-clouds low down in the sky.

And even among those who rejoiced in Jesus, an uneasy question sometimes stirred. He had preached that the Kingdom of God was at hand. Well then, where was it? Many had expected that the coming of God's Kingdom would be sudden and tremendous. Perhaps through a war for freedom from the Romans, with Jesus as the conqueror. Or perhaps it would come about through some other world-shaking event. But nothing of this sort was happening. Was Jesus, after all, *not* the Great Deliverer who had been expected?

Even John the Baptist was troubled. In his fearless preaching, he had dared to speak against the sins not only of ordinary people but of the great and powerful. He had denounced Herod Antipas, the ruler of Galilee, because this Herod had married his own brother's wife; so Herod had arrested John and shut him up in prison. Now John began to wonder what there was to hope for. He sent some of his disciples to Jesus to ask him, "Are you the One that is to come, or shall we look for another?"

Jesus answered, "Go and tell John what you have seen and heard: the blind receive their sight, the lame walk, lepers are cleansed and the deaf hear, and the dead are raised up, and the poor have the good news preached to them. And blessed is he who takes no offense in me."

When John the Baptist's disciples had gone away, Jesus spoke to the people around him about John—about his greatness, and also about what John had not yet understood.

When they went out into the wilderness where John was preaching, he asked them, what did they expect to find? A man in fine, soft clothes? No, if they had expected *that* they would have looked in kings' palaces. Well then, did they want to find there a man who could be blown this way and that, like a reed shaken in the wind? Or were they looking for a true prophet? If they were, they had surely found one. A prophet, yes, and more than a prophet: God's special messenger to bid men be ready for the coming of his Kingdom. "I tell you," Jesus said, "among those born of women there has risen no one greater than John the Baptist." And then he said this: "Yet who is least in the Kingdom of God is greater than he."

What did he mean by that, the people wondered? Not all of them understood him when he went on to say: "From the days of John the Baptist until now the Kingdom of heaven has suffered violence, and men of violence take it by force." Who indeed can say that he understands all that was in the mind of Jesus? But it may be that he was thinking of those who had been excited by John's preaching to believe that the Kingdom of God could be brought into the world by a war which they would unleash, or by some other fierce action of their own. Yet the truth was that God's Kingdom could come only when men gave their hearts completely to God and allowed him to cleanse them of their pride and hate, and to put into them the spirit they had seen in Jesus.

But that was what many were not ready to accept. To get the new and different kind of world they wanted by some quick violence—that sounded possible; but to have to *be* different themselves—that was another matter. There were plenty of people who wanted to have God work *for* them, but not to work *in* them. They had not come to the point of being willing to repent of their own sins.

Herod, having imprisoned John the Baptist, now added a worse wrong to those of which he had been already guilty. On his birthday he had a great banquet in his palace; and Herodias, his brother's wife, whom he had married, instructed her daughter to dance before the guests. Herod may have drunk too much, so that when he talked he said more than he meant to say. The dancing of Herodias' daughter pleased him and all his guests completely. He would show her now his royal favor. "What would you like to have?" he called out to her. "Ask me for anything you want, and you shall have it."

The girl went and talked with her mother. Now Herodias knew what John the Baptist had said of her and of Herod, and she hated John with a deadly hatred. "Go back to Herod," she said, "and tell him that what you want is the head of John the Baptist cut off and brought to you on a dish." So that is what the girl went and told the king.

Herod was shocked. He had put John in prison, but he had not meant to kill him. But he had made a promise, and, because all these guests at his banquet table had heard him, he was ashamed to take it back. He sent an order to the prison that John should be beheaded. And so John was put to death, and his head brought to satisfy Herodias.

About that time Herod began to hear of Jesus and of his mighty works among the people. A superstitious fear rose up in him. "This must be John the Baptist risen from the dead!", he said. He would be uneasy now as long as Jesus was in Galilee.

Some of the Pharisees, who had their own reasons for wanting to get rid of Jesus, came to him one day and told him, "Herod wants to kill you." Jesus answered, "Go and tell that fox: Behold, I cast out demons and perform cures today and tomorrow, and the third day I finish my course. Nevertheless, I must go on my way today and tomorrow and the day following."

He began to see now that the days ahead might be short. The number of those who chose to be his enemies was growing.

Jesus took the disciples with him to a town north of the Lake of Galilee, called Caesarea Philippi. The time had come to find out what they had begun to understand. He asked them what the people were saying about him.

The disciples answered that some said—like Herod—that he was John the Baptist risen from the dead. Some said he was Elijah come again. And some could not say exactly who they thought he was, except that he must be a prophet.

"But who do *you* say I am?" asked Jesus.

Then Simon Peter looked at him, and suddenly a thought that he had never dared to speak before—perhaps never *had* before—burst into words. "You are the Christ!" he said.

Jesus knew that the people had their own ideas of what the Christ, or the Messiah, would be when he should come. Many of them believed, and hoped, that he would be a firebrand to kindle war. If they heard that Jesus' disciples were calling him the Messiah, they would expect of him exactly what he was determined not to be. So when they talked to others they were not to use that name of him.

Then he told them something which left them grief-stricken and speechless. He told them that the chief men of the church in Israel would reject him—as they had begun to do already;

and that when he went up to Jerusalem, where the ruling priests were set against him, he would be killed.

Again it was Peter who first found his voice. With all his might he protested—that Jesus did not mean what he had said, that he *could* not mean it.

But Jesus rebuked Peter. Peter was echoing the same temptation to choose safety that the voice of Satan had brought during the temptation in the wilderness. It was the choice which all people who thought they had common sense would agree with, but it did not measure up to the great purpose of God. The salvation that God intended might have to be won through suffering. "Get behind me," he said to Peter, as he had said to the tempter in the wilderness. "You are not on the side of God, but of men."

Then he began to teach the disciples what, from that day on, they would need to learn. If they were to follow their Master, they must be ready to make the hard choice instead of the easy one. "Whoever would save his life," he said, "will lose it; and whoever loses his life for my sake and the gospel's, will save it."

The time for heroic commitment now had come.

CHAPTER EIGHTEEN

Jesus Sets His Face Toward Jerusalem

For Jesus, the certainty of danger ahead did not cast a shadow on his spirit. Instead, there came to him the supporting power of God which clothed him with a glory that some of the disciples would never afterwards forget.

He took with him Peter and James and John, and went up onto a mountain to pray; and there, in the words of the Gospels, "He was transfigured before them." As they looked at him, his face and his whole form were as though a light was shining through. Beholding him there they were speechless with awe, for it seemed to them that great figures from the heavenly world had come to stand beside him—Moses, the lawgiver, and Elijah, the mightiest of the prophets. Then presently Peter, hardly knowing what he said, found voice to stammer: "Master it is well that we are here. Let us make three booths, one for you and one for Moses and one for Elijah." But even as he spoke a cloud drifted across the mountain top, and when they looked again they saw Jesus there alone.

If only they could stay in that holy place forever, the disciples may have wished. But for Jesus then, as always, the closer he came to God in solitude and prayer the more sure he was to go back to meet the needs of people. He led the three disciples down from the mountain; and when they had reached the valley, they saw the rest of the disciples, surrounded by a crowd. In their midst was a man who had brought his afflicted son. He said that the boy had convulsions, which made him fall down and foam at the mouth and all his muscles tighten. He said he had asked the disciples to heal him, but they had not been able.

"How long has he been this way?" asked Jesus.

"Ever since he was a child," the father said. "But if you can do anything, have pity on us and help us."

"If you can!" Jesus repeated. This poor troubled man who was appealing to him wanted to have faith, but he did not fully have it. "All things are possible to him who believes," said Jesus; and the man answered desperately, "I believe; help my unbelief!"

Then Jesus turned to the afflicted boy. He was trembling and twisting as though some evil spirit were in him. "Come out of him," said Jesus, "and never enter him again." And though the boy gave a terrible cry and fell down as though he were dead, Jesus took his hand and lifted him up, and he was cured.

When they were alone again, the disciples asked Jesus why they had not been able to heal the afflicted boy. He said that kind of healing was possible only when one had prayed very much. And perhaps he felt that the disciples, or some of them, might be more interested in having the credit of being able to heal than they were in the pitiful people who needed to be healed.

One day on the road he heard them disputing. When they came into the house in Capernaum he asked them what the argument was about. At first no one answered, for they were ashamed to admit that they had been arguing over which of them would be the greatest. Jesus' answer was one that would be hard to live up to, but one which they could never after-

wards forget. For he said, "If any one would be first, he must
be last of all, and servant of all."

All this happened in Galilee, but the time had come when
Jesus would leave his own country. Jerusalem was the capital,
and it was there that the message he had to bring from God
would matter most. It was called the Holy City, and this was
what it could truly be if it knew its opportunity. Yet there
were evil forces in Jerusalem, and it was a risk to go there. So
in the Gospel of Luke it is written that "Jesus set his face
to go to Jerusalem," but in the Gospel of Mark it is told also
that "those who followed were afraid."

The reports about Jesus had already spread beyond Galilee.
So as he went on his way now toward Jerusalem many people
hurried to see and hear him when they learned that he might
be coming near to where they lived. Some had only curiosity,
some had questions they wanted to ask, but some had real
desire for what he might bring to them of God.

One day a young man came running toward him. "Good
master," he cried, "what shall I do to inherit eternal life?"

"You know the Commandments," Jesus answered. "Do not
kill. Do not commit adultery. Do not steal. Do not bear false
witness. Honor your father and mother."

The young man said that he had kept all the Commandments since he was a child.

Jesus looked at him and loved him. Here was one who might
be a real disciple, and give his whole heart to the service of
God. But did he care enough to do that?

Jesus saw that he was very rich.

"You lack one thing," he said. "Go, sell all that you have,
and give it to the poor, and you will have treasure in heaven.
Then come and follow me."

The whole look of the young man changed. The eagerness

went out of his face. This was too much. He turned and went away, disappointed and sad.

"How hard it will be," said Jesus, "for those who have riches to enter the Kingdom of God."

The disciples were amazed. Here was this young man who seemed so fine, and yet he could not belong to the Kingdom of God. If such as he could not be saved, who could?

But Jesus knew that the time had now come for hard decisions; and he knew that anyone who had always had everything he wanted and had grown soft through self-indulgence would flinch from hard decisions, and that a person loaded with possessions could not get through the narrow gate. "It is easier for a camel to go through the eye of a needle," said Jesus, "than for a rich man to enter the Kingdom of God."

So, then—the disciples thought—Jesus has made it hopeless. There are some who will never get into the Kingdom of God, no matter how much they seem to want to. But Jesus answered that with God things that seem impossible are possible. If men wanted God enough, God could give them power to break the hold of anything which keeps them back from him.

Perhaps it was because of what this young man had missed that Jesus told this parable recorded in the Gospel of Luke:

There was a rich man who had land that brought forth plentifully. And he thought to himself, "What shall I do, for I have nowhere to store my crops?" And he said, "I will do this: I will pull down my barns, and build larger ones; and there I will store all my grain and my goods. And I will say to my soul, Soul, you have ample goods laid up for many years; take your ease, eat, drink, and be merry." But God said to him, "Fool! This night your soul is required of you; and the things you have prepared, whose will they be?"

So is he who lays up treasure for himself, and is not rich toward God.

Peter said, "We have left everything and followed you." Yes, they had, said Jesus. And they would gain far more than they had lost. It would not be the kind of gain that most people imagined. It would be living for something bigger and braver than they had ever known before. With its risks would come great rewards. "But," Jesus reminded them, "many that are first will be last, and the last first."

The disciples heard those words of Jesus, but they were slow to take them in. If they had given up a great deal to follow Jesus, then surely—they thought—they would have their rewards as Jesus said. And perhaps those rewards would be so dazzling that what they had left behind would seem as nothing.

Two of them, James and John, came to Jesus and they said there was something they wanted to ask him to do for them, and would he do it?

"What do you want me to do for you?" Jesus answered.

Then they let him know what they had in mind. Jesus seemed to them so wonderful that nothing was too great to happen. Power and glory would belong to him, and that power and glory would be as in the kingdoms of the world they knew. Jesus would sit on a throne and rule. So they asked him if, when this came true, they could have the places next to him, one on his right hand and the other on his left.

But Jesus said to them, "You do not know what you are asking. Are you able to drink the cup that I drink, or to be baptized with the baptism with which I am baptized?"

That answer turned all that they had been thinking upside down. It was not a question now of getting the places of highest honor. It was a question of how much they would dare, and of whether they were ready to go into unlimited danger for Jesus' sake. "The cup" that he would drink was the cup of suffering, and the baptism he was baptized with was faithfulness to God's purpose, no matter what it cost.

They made a brave answer—an answer that at least they wanted to live up to. Could they drink of the cup and be baptized with his baptism? Yes, they said, they could.

The other disciples heard what had happened and they were indignant against James and John. These two had tried to get in first to gain the honors which secretly all of them might have been coveting. So Jesus saw that all of them needed to learn that the kind of greatness which came with following him was completely different from the selfish notions they had. They saw the way that kings and emperors generally ruled— lording over people for their own benefit. "But it shall not be so among you," he said. "Whoever would be great among you must be your servant, and whoever would be first among you must be slave of all. For the Son of man also came not to be served but to serve, and to give his life as a ransom for many."

CHAPTER NINETEEN

The Stern Tests of Discipleship

To GIVE his life—that was what Jesus was ready to do, and what increasingly he knew that he might need to do. As he went on toward Jerusalem, he made it clear that no one looking only for an easy road should come with him. Several men on different days had seemed all full of eagerness to join the company of his disciples. But they wanted to wait and start tomorrow. Could they go home first and attend to this and that? They could not, said Jesus. It was a time for clear decision. "No one who puts his hand to the plow and looks back is fit for the Kingdom of God," he said.

On another day he told the parable, recorded in the Gospel of Matthew, of the ten bridesmaids, five of whom were wise and five were foolish. They had started out with their lamps in the evening to meet a wedding procession and to go with it to the wedding feast. But there was a long delay, and they went to sleep. Then, about midnight, when suddenly there was a cry "The bridegroom is coming," the foolish five, who had been too careless to make sure they had plenty of oil, found that their lamps had gone out. They hurried here and there to beg or borrow or buy more oil, but it was too late to find any. And when at length they came to the house where the guests were at the wedding supper and knocked and called,

The man blind from birth to whom Jesus said, "Go, wash in the pool of Siloam." So he went and washed, and to his amazement he could see.

And there appeared Elijah with Moses, talking to Jesus.

Jesus driving the money-changers out of the Temple.

Judas immediately went out; and it was night.

they could not get in. "The door was shut." In those four solemn words Jesus made it plain that for those who had only carelessly thought that they wanted to enter the Kingdom of God, there might come the time when it would be too late.

The heedless and the half-hearted could not find the way into the Kingdom of God. And neither could those who thought they had arrived there already. That was the trouble with some of the scribes and Pharisees. They thought they must be important persons in God's sight because they seemed so important to the ordinary people. Didn't everybody know their reputation? They, and their fathers before them, had always behaved as proper persons should. If any person looked at the Scriptures, couldn't he see that they were the Chosen People to whom God had made his promises? But Jesus said that often it would be the humble people, and the unexpected, who would be found in the Kingdom of God, and not the self-righteous ones who were so sure that they belonged there. "I tell you," Jesus said, "many will come from East and West and sit at table with Abraham, Isaac and Jacob in the Kingdom of heaven, while the sons of the Kingdom will be thrown into the outer darkness."

What that meant was made more plain one day when a lawyer came to him with what he thought was a hard question. He wanted to know what were the greatest Commandments of God. The lawyer supposed it might be hard for Jesus to choose among them all. But Jesus made him see that all God's Commandments could be summed up into two. "You shall love the Lord your God with all your heart, and with all your soul, and with all your strength, and with all your mind; and you shall love your neighbor as yourself."

"Yes," said the lawyer, "but who is my neighbor?"

He thought that Jesus might give him an answer that he could live up to without too much trouble. His neighbor might be the person who lived next door, or his relatives or his friends; people, anyhow, who belonged in some special way to him. If he did his duty toward them, he would not have to worry about the rest.

But Jesus gave him an answer that astonished him.

A man was going down from Jerusalem to Jericho, said Jesus, and he fell among robbers. They stripped him and beat him and left him half dead.

Now by chance a priest was going down that road; and when he saw the man lying there, he went by on the other side. Presently along came a Levite—a man, who like the priest, spent his life carrying on the worship in the Temple. When the Levite caught sight of the wounded man, he did what the priest had done. He gave one look and hurried by. But then came another man, a Samaritan. When he saw the man whom the robbers had beaten, he had pity on him, went to his side, and dressed his wounds. Then he put the wounded man on his own mount that he had been riding, carried him to an inn, and told the innkeeper to take care of him—and he would pay the charges.

"Which of these three," Jesus asked, "do you think proved neighbor to the man who fell among the robbers?"

There was nothing for the scribe to answer except, "The one who showed mercy on him." Then Jesus said: "Go and do likewise." And the point was that the man who had showed mercy was a Samaritan, one of the people for whom most Jews had nothing but contempt. This Samaritan had showed more of God in his behavior than the priest and Levite who made a business of seeming to be religious. In the sight of God it was true again that "many that are first will be last, and the last first."

In one of the greatest of his parables Jesus made plain what sort of people it was who might be lost, and what sort saved. In his words there was a sound as awful as though the bells of judgment rang.

"When the Son of man comes in his glory," he said, "and all the angels with him, then will he sit on his glorious throne. Before him will be gathered all the nations, and he will separate them one from another as a shepherd separates the sheep from the goats."

So the parable began; and then Jesus went on to describe what will happen on that Judgment Day. To those on his right hand he will say, "Come O blessed of my Father, inherit the Kingdom prepared for you from the foundation of the world. For I was hungry and you gave me food, I was thirsty and you gave me drink, I was a stranger and you welcomed me, I was naked and you clothed me, I was sick and you visited me, I was in prison and you came to me."

Then in astonishment they will ask the Lord how or when they could ever have done all this for him; and he will answer, "As you did it to one of the least of these my brethren, you did it to me."

But those on his left hand he will send away to shame and darkness, because they did nothing for him when he was in distress. In shocked amazement they will protest that they never could have neglected him. If they had ever seen him hungry, or thirsty or cold or homeless or in prison, they would surely have responded then. But he will answer, "As you did it not to one of the least of these, you did it not to me."

What Jesus meant in that parable of the Judgment no one could mistake. The important thing which counts with God is not what men do only in those great moments when they imagine that God is watching. It is in what they do in the common times and for the little people to whom their compassion goes out with no thought of getting credit for it.

Jesus told something else that needed to be heard by those who trusted in themselves and who were righteous and despised others.

"Two men," he said, "went up into the Temple to pray, one

a Pharisee and the other a tax collector. The Pharisee stood and prayed thus with himself, 'God, I thank thee that I am not like other men, extortioners, unjust, adulterers, or even like this tax collector. I fast twice a week, I give tithes of all that I get.' But the tax-collector, standing far off, would not even lift up his eyes to heaven, but beat his breast, saying 'God, be merciful to me a sinner!' I tell you, this man went down to his house justified rather than the other; for every one who exalts himself will be humbled, but he who humbles himself will be exalted."

CHAPTER TWENTY

Jesus Enters the Perilous City

ON HIS WAY toward Jerusalem, Jesus had come to the edge of the city of Jericho. On the road outside the city there sat a blind man, begging. His ears caught the sound of many footsteps as a crowd hurried out at the news that Jesus was coming. "What is happening?" he asked of those who would pause long enough to listen to him. And they called back, "Jesus of Nazareth is passing by!"

"Jesus, Son of David," he cried, "have mercy on me!"

The people who lined the road in front of him told him to keep still, but he cried out all the more. "Son of David, have mercy on me!"

Jesus stopped. He told his disciples to go and bring the man who was calling. When the blind man came near, Jesus said, "What do you want me to do for you?" And he answered, "Lord, let me receive my sight!"

"Receive your sight," said Jesus; "your faith has made you well." Then instantly the blind man could see again, and he followed Jesus, glorifying God.

By the time Jesus had come into Jericho, the crowd around him had grown so great that the streets were full. Now there was a little man, named Zacchaeus, who was a tax-collector— as Matthew, one of the disciples, had also been. Zacchaeus was short, and so he had no chance of seeing over the heads of the crowd, and because he was a tax-collector it was certain that no one would make room and let him through. So Zacchaeus climbed up into a tree in order that he might see Jesus.

When Jesus came near he looked up to where Zacchaeus was. Those quick eyes of his saw in Zacchaeus' eyes a longing that the crowd would not have understood. To the astonishment of the people he said, "Zacchaeus, make haste and come down; for I must stay at your house today."

At Zacchaeus' house! That was the last place those who considered themselves to be the best people would have expected Jesus to want to stay. They could hardly believe it. "He is going in to be the guest of a man who is a sinner," they said.

But Jesus did not judge a man by his reputation. He knew that sometimes in the most unexpected person there was a hunger for goodness and for God. He had seen that in Zacchaeus. And after Jesus had come into Zacchaeus' house, Zacchaeus cried, "Behold, Lord, the half of my goods I give to the poor; and if I have defrauded anyone of anything, I restore it four times over."

Here was a man, said Jesus, who was more truly a son of Abraham than some of the Pharisees and scribes who were so sure that they belonged to the Chosen People. Zacchaeus might

have been in a bad business, but in his heart he had always been concerned with something better. And now in the presence of Jesus he had a new understanding of the forgiving love of God. "Today," said Jesus, "salvation has come to this house. For the Son of man came to seek and to save that which was lost."

From Jericho Jesus went on toward Jerusalem. Jericho lay in a green oasis in the valley of the Jordan River; from there the steep road climbed up toward the heights. There, at length, could be caught the first breath-taking view of what had so long been thought of as the Holy City. "Our feet shall stand within thy gates, O Jerusalem. . . . Glorious things are spoken of thee, O city of God"—such were the joyful words that the throngs of pilgrims sang year after year when they came up to Jerusalem for the great feasts such as the Passover. It was nearly time for the Passover now, and Jesus may have been remembering the wonder and the gladness that were in his heart when he was twelve years old, and had come to a Passover for the first time. His love for all that Jerusalem was meant to be was even deeper now, but so was his knowledge of how often Jerusalem had forgotten God. The leaders of the church were there, but they were the men who most of all needed to repent of their pride and hardness before they could really want the Kingdom of God. He had come now to preach the gospel. But who could tell whether they would listen?

On and up the road he went, with his disciples round him, until they came to the crest of the hill called Olivet. There suddenly, across a little valley that lay between, with the great gates and walls and golden roof of the Temple glistening against the sky, was Jerusalem.

Jesus stopped near the little village of Bethany. He told the disciples to go into the village and at a certain place they would find a colt tied. They were to untie the colt and bring it to him, and say to the man to whom the colt belonged, "The Lord has need of it."

The disciples brought the colt, and Jesus sat upon it. And now because the news had spread that he was near, a crowd was flocking out from Jerusalem. Some of them were pilgrims from Galilee who had come up to Jerusalem for the Passover. When they saw Jesus, their welcome rose to a great excitement. With the disciples they threw down branches of fresh leaves and even their garments to make a royal road for Jesus to ride upon. And they shouted, "Blessed be the King who comes in the name of the Lord, and glory in the highest!"

So the common people welcomed Jesus. But more important men in Jerusalem did not welcome him. The chief priests and other leaders of the Jewish church had already been made suspicious by reports that had come to them from Galilee. This Jesus of Nazareth whom so many people followed—who

was he, and what was the reason for the excitement that gathered round him? Now here he was in Jerusalem, when the
city was filled with the Passover crowd. There might be trouble
—trouble which could get out of control.

When the Romans had conquered a country they were quick
to put down anything that looked like rebellion or disorder.
But in smaller matters they generally left the government in
the hands of men who belonged to the subject people. In the
land of Judea (the province to which Jerusalem belonged)
there was a Roman governor, Pontius Pilate. But there was
also a council of priests called the Sanhedrin; and the Sanhedrin was held responsible for what happened in Jerusalem.
The chief priest, and the head of the Sanhedrin, was Caiaphas.
A powerful man he was, with fixed ideas, who could be merciless.

Jesus knew of Caiaphas. He knew that this priest who was
supposed to be devoted to the worship of God was more devoted to his own pride of office. To see that everybody obeyed
the rulings of the Sanhedrin, and that no dangerous ideas
should arise—that was what Caiaphas was concerned about.
He would keep up the forms of religion, but he would not
endure any preaching of religion that might create a disturbance. From what he had heard about Jesus, he had already
begun to be against him. To Caiaphas the crowds which
flocked around Jesus meant a threat. "If we let him go on
thus," he said angrily to the Sanhedrin, "every one will believe
in him, and the Romans will come and destroy both our holy
place and our nation."

Jesus understood what he would be facing. The "Holy City"
was not holy. The men who ought to have been the teachers
of God's righteousness could not be trusted. In the end, they
would have sufficient power to twist the minds of the people
to suit their own purposes. So the welcome which had rung
so loudly on Olivet might last only for a day. "O Jerusalem,

Jerusalem," Jesus said, "killing the prophets and stoning those who are sent to you! How often would I have gathered your children together as a hen gathers her brood under her wings, and you would not!"

CHAPTER TWENTY-ONE

The Antagonism Hardens

N OW BEGAN the last crowded week of Jesus' life, when what he had told the disciples at Caesarea Philippi would come true. He would be "rejected by the elders and the chief priests and the scribes, and put to death."

On the morning after his entrance into Jerusalem, which is now remembered as "Palm Sunday," Jesus went into the courts of the Temple in Jerusalem. What he saw about him made righteous anger burn within him. At the center of the Temple was the "Holy of Holies," the shrine of inmost silence which was meant to express the unspeakable greatness of God. Yet certain places in the Temple's outer courts had been rented out by the priests to traders and money-changers who haggled with the worshippers who came to buy what was needed for the Temple sacrifices. The corridors echoed with the fluttering of pigeons, the bleating of sheep, and the noise of greedy bargaining. "It is written," said Jesus, "that my house shall be a house of prayer; but you have made it a den of robbers!" And, before anyone knew what was happening, he came upon the traders like the wrath of God, overturning their money tables and driving them and their animals before him out of the Temple.

Now it was certain that Jesus would have new enemies. What, the traders wanted to know, did Jesus have to do with what went on in the Temple? Only Caiaphas and the other priests had authority, and the priests had sold them the right to traffic there. It was an outrage—so they thought—that Jesus should dare to break up their businesses. They would be quick enough to join with the Sanhedrin if the chance came to get rid of Jesus.

The next day and the day following Jesus came back to the Temple courts and taught the crowds that immediately gathered round him. Wherever he saw anything good and beautiful, he was glad of it, and called attention to it. Once he was watching the people who came up to drop their offerings in one of the boxes for the Temple treasury. Among them were rich men who put in large amounts. Then came a poor widow, who gave two small copper coins. That poor widow, said Jesus, had put in more than all the others who were making larger contributions. They had given out of their abundance, but she had given out of her poverty and had put in all she had.

People came and asked Jesus all sorts of questions. When these questions came out of men's hearts, he answered them with the patient gentleness he always had for those who were ready to listen to the gospel of the love of God. But he could be quick and stern with those whose questions were only meant to trap him.

Some of the priests and scribes looked for him in the Temple, and they demanded to know by what right he did what he had been doing. Who gave him authority?

"I will ask you one question," said Jesus. "Answer that, and then I will tell you what is my authority." Let them tell him what they thought of the work of John the Baptist. Did his baptizing have in it the power of God, or was it only something that any ordinary person might have done. "Was it from heaven, or from man?"

They put their heads together and argued, but they could not come up with any answer. Angrily they admitted to one another that they themselves were trapped. If they said that John's baptism was only "from men," they were afraid of the crowd, for the people believed that John was a great prophet. But if they said "From heaven," then Jesus would ask why they had not listened to him. "We do not know," they muttered sullenly.

Well, if they did not know about John's authority, said Jesus, there was no use for him to tell them about his. His questioners went away trying not to let their faces show what they knew was a fact—that they had been made to look foolish before the people.

Another group of them tried again. They began in a way that sounded most respectful. "Teacher," they said, "we know that you are true and care for no man; for you do not regard the position of men, but truly teach the way of God." But then came the tricky question which they thought would put Jesus in trouble, whichever way he answered it. "Is it lawful to pay taxes to Caesar, or not?"

If he said, yes, it was right to pay the Roman taxes, all the people, who hated Rome, would be offended. If he said no, then the Roman governor would have something quick and merciless to say.

Jesus saw in an instant what their purpose was. "Bring me a coin," he said. They brought him one, and he held it up—a Roman coin with the profile of the Roman emperor stamped upon it.

"Whose likeness and inscription is this?" he asked. "Caesar's," they answered. Then said Jesus, "Render to Caesar the things that are Caesar's, and to God the things that are God's."

The scribes and Pharisees had been caught again in what

they thought was a clever trap they had laid for Jesus. The crowd was delighted. But these men who had been outwitted would be all the more dangerous now. Twice they had been made ridiculous, and that was more than they could stand. From now on, there was nothing they would not do to settle the score with Jesus.

Jesus knew what was in their hearts. Their sullen anger made it sure that the message he had come to bring from God would be rejected, and that his own death could not be far away. So he put what he chose to say into a parable:

There was a man, Jesus said, who had a vineyard and rented it out to tenants who were to grow its fruit for him. When the crop was due to be gathered and the rent due to be paid, he sent his servant to receive it, but the men who had the vineyard took the servant and beat him and sent him away empty-handed. A second time, and a third time, and even a fourth they did that, until the lord of the vineyard determined to send his own son. "They will respect him," he said. But when the tenants saw him they said to one another, "This is the heir. Come, let us kill him, and then the inheritance will belong to us." So they killed him, and cast his body outside the vineyard wall.

The terrible meaning of that parable was plain. Jerusalem, which again and again had put to death God's prophets, would kill also the Son. The priests and rulers were like the tenants in possession of the vineyard. And what was the final message of the parable? It was this: The Lord of the vineyard must come with dreadful judgment upon the men who had abused their privilege. He would sweep them out, and put others in their place.

So that was what would happen to Jerusalem. Looking at the city now, Jesus knew that it was doomed. A dreadful time was coming when the city would be destroyed with war and bloodshed, and all the magnificence of its walls and buildings smashed until hardly one stone would be left upon another.

But Caiaphas and the other priests did not believe that. They still had power in their hands. And they thought that all would be well with them, and others like them, if they could get rid of Jesus.

CHAPTER TWENTY-TWO

The Betrayal,
and the Last Supper

A S THE DANGER increased, those who had been Jesus' closest friends meant more to him than ever. In the evenings now he went out to the little village of Bethany, near Jerusalem. There he stayed at the house of two sisters, Martha and Mary—of whose brother, Lazarus, the Gospel of John tells that he was raised from the dead.

Martha was the housekeeper, and she was eager to give Jesus the best supper that could possibly be prepared. As she hurried about, she almost lost her temper because of all the things she had set herself to do—and had to do alone. For there was Mary, who was not helping, but sitting at the feet of Jesus listening to him.

Martha was annoyed. She said to Jesus, "Lord, don't you care that my sister has left me to do all the work. Tell her then to help me."

Jesus looked at her with gentle understanding of her good

intentions, but he must also let her see that she was making a
mistake. "Martha, Martha," he said, "you are anxious and
troubled about many things." But something she had not
thought about was more important, and that was the kind of
welcome Mary had given him. "One thing is needful," he

said. "Mary has chosen the good portion, which shall not be
taken away from her." What he might have for supper did not
so greatly matter; what did matter was that those who loved
him should take time to learn what was happening and about
to happen in Jerusalem; and what it meant for him and for
them.

The twelve disciples who had followed him all the way from
Galilee were devoted to him—all except one. It was true that
even the best of them were slow to understand Jesus, but now
there was one who had grown bitter about what he thought he
foresaw. This was Judas Iscariot.

What, Judas began to ask himself, had been the use of following Jesus? He may have thought in the beginning—as James and John did—that Jesus would set up a kingdom in which there would be power and honor for his followers. But now all the signs pointed the other way. Judas could see that the enemies of Jesus would be stronger than his friends. It was true, as Jesus had foretold and as the disciples had not believed, that Jesus might be rejected and killed. So what was the reward for having followed him? What but danger and the risk of death? James and John had been great-hearted enough to measure up to that when they had to make their choice. But not Judas. He was not going to let Jesus carry him along to what looked like certain destruction. He would change sides while there was time.

So, one night when no one saw him, Judas went to Caiaphas and the priests. He knew that they would arrest Jesus if they could. They had not yet dared to try, for they were afraid that if the people heard of it in advance there would be violence. But if they could find a way to arrest him secretly—that was what they needed. And Judas, being one of the disciples and being familiar with all of Jesus' movements, was the man who could let them know.

They were glad then to have Judas brought in when he came knocking secretly at the high priest's door. Judas said that he had his reasons for deserting Jesus and that he would soon let them know the time and place, away from the notice of the crowd, where they could find Jesus. Well then, declared Caiaphas and his priests, they would strike a bargain. And they handed Judas thirty pieces of silver as his reward.

The week went on, and it was time to make ready for the Passover. Jesus sent two of the disciples into the city, telling them to look for a certain house with a large upper room. In that room he and the other disciples would meet them for the Passover supper. So in the evening he came with the rest of the twelve.

For all the people of Israel, the Passover was the great festival of proud thanksgiving, for it was the memorial of the deliverance of their forefathers from their bondage in the land of Egypt. When men kept the Passover they felt again that they were members of the Chosen People of God. Moses had led their fathers to freedom in the Promised Land, even when all the signs seemed to indicate that he would fail. And now, as Jesus brought them together, most of the disciples believed that the power of God might be shown again in some wondrous way.

Indeed, that power *would* show itself for the saving of the souls of men, and in a manner beyond their dreams; but it would not be the way their human desires might have chosen. There would be suffering first, and darkness, and what would seem to be disaster.

Jesus took up the loaf of bread for the Passover supper, blessed and broke it, and gave it to the disciples. He took the cup of wine, gave thanks and passed it to them, and they all drank from the one cup. This would be his Last Supper with them, he said, and the Passover meal now would mean that they belonged to him, and that all he lived for and might die for would belong to them. "This is my body," he said, as he gave them the bread. And, as he gave them the cup from which they drank, he said: "This is my blood of the Covenant."

Then, as they sat hushed and awed, he said a shocking thing: "One of you will betray me."

Judas knew who that one was. But for the other disciples is was past belief that one of them who had followed him from Galilee, who sat with him now at the Passover table—in the group whom he had trusted—one of *them* would betray him? No, it could not be!

Yet that was that Jesus had said. And, wondering wretchedly whether they might be greater cowards than they had ever wanted to believe, the disciples began to ask who it could be. It was as though each one were begging him to say that *he* was not the one. "Not I, Master, not I! Tell me that you don't mean me!"

But Jesus answered, "It is one of the twelve, who is dipping bread in the same dish with me."

Judas Iscariot could not stand the guilty secret that he carried in his own heart. He got up immediately from the table and went out; and it was night.

Simon Peter cried that whatever anyone else might do, he would never leave Jesus. "Lord, I am ready to go with you to prison and to death," he promised. But Jesus checked him. "I tell you, Peter," he said, "the cock will not crow twice this day until you deny three times that you even know me." "If I must die with you, I will not deny you," Peter protested; and all the others said the same. With all their might they wanted to believe that, and they were trying to banish by brave words the fear which stirred miserably within them.

CHAPTER TWENTY-THREE

In Gethsemane,
and in Caiaphas' Court

As THE LAST SUPPER drew to a close, Jesus and the disciples
sang a hymn, and then Jesus said that it was time to go.
Into the dark street, through which Judas had already gone,
Jesus led the others—out beyond the city walls to a place called
the Garden of Gethsemane. Here, at various times, he had
been accustomed to going among the olive trees to pray. He
left the disciples at the edge of the garden, while he went
deeper among the trees.

He was sure now of what would happen. He knew what
was in the heart of Judas. If one of his own disciples betrayed
him, the chief priests and others in Jerusalem who wanted
his death would have their way. It was as though moral darkness had descended upon the earth, and evil had come to its
appointed hour. Tomorrow a cross might wait for him. The
physical suffering would be dreadful then. But now in Gethsemane Jesus knew another suffering: the consciousness that
his own people of Israel had rejected the love of God through
stubbornness and pride, the consequences of which he would
take upon himself.

And what of all that he had set out to do? If he went now,
could the disciples stand alone? Would the forces of wickedness scatter them, so that nothing would be left? *"Abba,*

Father," he prayed, "all things are possible to thee; remove this cup from me."

But then he said, "Not what I will, but what thou wilt."

He came back to where he had left the disciples, and he found that they were asleep. He looked at Simon Peter, and he said to him, "Couldn't you watch with me one hour? Watch and pray, that you may not enter into temptation. The spirit indeed is willing, but the flesh is weak."

Twice more he went apart among the trees, and knelt down in his lonely agony of prayer; and when he returned, he saw that the disciples were asleep again. When he came the third time, he woke them. "It is enough," he said, "the hour has come. The Son of Man is betrayed into the hands of sinners. Rise, let us be going. See, my betrayer is at hand."

At that moment Judas came, at the head of a company of armed men sent by the chief priests and the elders. Because it would be dark under the trees of the garden, Judas had arranged a sign by which they could know which one was Jesus. "The one I shall kiss is the man," he said, "seize him, and lead him away."

"Master!" he said when he saw Jesus, and he went up to him and kissed him.

The armed guard laid hold of Jesus to take him away. "This is your hour, and the power of darkness," Jesus said. And the disciples fled.

Into Jerusalem through streets that were empty now, for it was late, Jesus was led to the high priest's house, where the council of the elders had been assembled. Witnesses were brought in to testify to this and that which they claimed to have heard him say and to have seen him do. But they contradicted one another and Caiaphas, the high priest, saw that this trial he wanted to carry through was getting nowhere.

Angrily then he turned to Jesus. "Have you no answer to make?" he demanded; but Jesus was silent. Once more the high priest tried. "Are you the Christ?" he asked. "The Son of the Blessed?"

Then Jesus answered: "I am; and you will see the Son of Man sitting at the right hand of the Power, and coming with the clouds of heaven!"

Now the high priest had got from Jesus the words that would serve his purpose better than any other testimony. "You have heard his blasphemy!" he shouted to the council. "What further testimony do we need?" He took hold of his own mantle and tore it as a sign of horror. Jesus had claimed to be the Messiah, the one who stood next to God himself.

"What is your decision?" he asked the council. They cried that Jesus should be put to death. The guards who stood around him struck him, and the members of the council spat upon him in their disgust.

Where were the disciples now? They had fled from the Garden of Gethsemane. Only one of them had followed close enough to find out what was happening. Peter had got into the courtyard of the high priest's house, thinking that nobody would notice him in the crowd that was milling about. But there was a fire in the midst of the courtyard, and as Peter drew near to warm himself, one of the high priest's maid-servants recognized him in the light that fell upon his face.

"You were with the Nazarene, Jesus," she declared.

Peter denied it. He said he didn't know what she was talking about; and he tried to slip away toward the gate.

Somewhere, out in the night that was changing to the break of day, a cock crowed.

But the maid-servant caught sight of him again and she said to those who were standing near, "This man is one of them."

Once more Peter denied it, but the bystanders agreed with the maid-servant. "Yes, you are one of them," they insisted, "for the way you talk shows that you are a Galilean."

This time Peter began to curse and swear that he did not even know who Jesus was.

The cock crowed again.

Then Peter remembered how Jesus had said to him, "Before the cock crows twice, you will deny me three times." And he broke down and wept.

CHAPTER TWENTY-FOUR

The Trial Before Pilate, and the Crucifixion

═══════════════════════════════════════

THE PRIESTS and the elders consulted as to what they should do. They had declared that Jesus had spoken blasphemy, and therefore by Jewish law he was guilty of death. But under the Roman rule their council had no power to carry out a death sentence. Only the Roman governor could order death.

So, as soon as it was morning, they led Jesus to the court of Pontius Pilate. Pilate came out to meet them. He saw that they had brought a prisoner. "What accusation do you bring against this man?" he demanded.

Caiaphas and the other priests did not want to have to explain. They knew that their Jewish judgments might not sound convincing to the Roman. "If this man were not an evil-doer, we would not have handed him over," they answered. They had accused him, and that ought to be enough.

Pilate replied contemptuously. "If you have tried him, very well then, judge him according to your law." But the priests had to admit that what they wanted was to put Jesus to death, and they could not do that without a Roman verdict.

Pilate, therefore, had the trial on his hands. He brought Jesus in where he could question him. "Are you the King of the Jews?" he demanded. "Your own nation and the chief priests have handed you over to me. What have you done?"

Jesus answered that the kingship that belonged to him was not a thing that had to do with this world's violence. He had come, he said, to bear witness to the truth.

Pilate looked at him increduously. "What is truth?" he scoffed. As a Roman, he thought he knew what power was. But this talk of a kingdom of the truth seemed to him only empty words.

The whole matter of the charge against Jesus began to irritate him. He could make no sense of it. But he knew he was more drawn toward Jesus than toward his accusers. He brought Jesus back to the balcony above the courtyard where the priests and the crowd that had come with them were gathered. "I find no crime in him," he said.

But there was an angry murmur. Caiaphas and the council were determined now to have Jesus condemned. They had their own reasons, and there were other powerful men in Jerusalem who also had cause against Jesus and would back them up. The traders whom Jesus had driven out of the temple were full of bitter resentment toward him. Men like these were in Pilate's courtyard now, and they were in an ugly mood.

Pilate began to see that he was in increasing trouble. All that was just and decent in him put him on the side of the man he was supposed to judge, standing there so quietly and so unafraid. But the crowd before him was restless.

Pilate would pretend to do a favor for the priests and those who followed them. He had heard that Jesus had been called the Messiah. He supposed that all Jewish people would welcome the Messiah. Jesus had been brought to him as a prisoner to be punished, but there was a custom that at Passover time the governor should release some prisoner in honor of the feast. He would release Jesus. That ought to please the people. Was not the Messiah supposed to be some sort of king?

So he beckoned for silence, and said to Caiaphas and those

who stood about him. "Do you want me to release for you the King of the Jews?"

There was an angry shout. No, it was a different sort of prisoner they wanted released. Let him release Barabbas, who had been accused of murder.

"Then what shall I do with the man whom you call the King of the Jews?" asked Pilate. And there came back the furious cry, "Crucify him!"

Pilate was astonished. "Shall I crucify your King?" he demanded.

Caiaphas and the others had a quick and ready answer. The last thing they would put up with was the idea that Jesus was any king of theirs. But they saw their chance to trap Pilate because he had used that word. "If you release this man, you are not Caesar's friend," they cried; "everyone who makes himself a king sets himself against Caesar."

Pilate knew that he was caught. He had had trouble with these priests before. They had complained to the emperor about something he had done. If they complained again, and made a case against him, he might be ordered back to Rome. Now if he released Jesus, and if there should be a disturbance, he could be accused of deliberately setting free someone who was dangerous to Roman rule.

Furiously he commanded his soldiers to take Jesus away and scourge him. This they did; and while they were at it, they mocked him. "Hail, King of the Jews!" they laughed. And they found an old piece of purple cloth and put it about his shoulders like a royal robe; then they twisted a crown out of twigs from a thorn-bush and set it on his head.

When Jesus was brought back, Pilate led him out on the balcony, wearing the purple robe and the crown of thorns. If he could not get rid of these priests and the crowd which as a Roman he despised, he could insult them. "Here is your King!" he said.

"We have no king but Caesar," they shouted back. If Pilate chose to call Jesus a king and then to set him free, then let him take the consequences with the emperor. For they knew well that this was the one thing of which Pilate would be afraid.

Pilate hesitated. They had him in a corner, and he knew it. Well then, he demanded, what should he do with Jesus?

And again the furious cry broke out: "Crucify him, crucify him!"

"Bring me a basin of water," said Pilate to a servant; and there before the crowd he washed his hands of the whole affair. "You take him, then, and crucify him," he said.

So Pilate handed Jesus over to a guard of soldiers to be taken out and crucified, according to the will of Caiaphas and the Council.

Outside the walls of Jerusalem was a low hill called Golgotha (which means the place of a skull). It was to this place that Jesus now was led. With him were two others who also had been sentenced to crucifixion, men who had been condemned as thieves.

The wooden beams which were to be made into his cross had been laid on Jesus' shoulders. Bruised and bleeding as he was from the scourging by Pilate's soldiers, he fell beneath the weight. The centurion in command looked into the crowd that was following along and his eye fell upon a man named Simon of Cyrene, who had just come in from the country. He ordered him to carry part of the cross.

So the procession came to Golgotha—which is also called Calvary. There the crosses were set up. Jesus' hands and feet were nailed to the central one; and on either side of him one of the thieves was crucified.

Some of those who had been in Pilate's court and had demanded Jesus' death had followed to the hill, and then crowded as close as the soldiers would allow them to the foot

of Jesus' cross. They taunted him as he hung there. So he was the one who had done such great things! *He* was the one who was supposed to be the Messiah! *He* had saved other people. Well, let him show whether he could save himself. "Come down now from the cross," they jeered, "that we may see and believe."

But no passion of a mob could poison Jesus' spirit. "Father, forgive them," he prayed, "for they know not what they do."

One of the crucified thieves also began to revile him. "So you are the Christ!" he snarled. "Then why don't you save yourself, and save us?"

But the other thief looked at Jesus and knew that he had never seen anyone like this before. There was something in this thief, wicked though he was, which recognized goodness and reached out for God. It was a shame that the first thief had spoken as he did to Jesus. "We deserve what we have got," the second thief said. "But this man is innocent." And then as he turned his head toward Jesus, a great awe and admiration filled him when he saw the look in Jesus' eyes. "Remember me," he cried, "when you come into your kingly power!"

"Today," said Jesus, "you will be with me in Paradise."

The hours went by, and the torture of the nails grew worse. Round the foot of the cross the soldiers gambled to see who should have the clothes that had belonged to Jesus. His mother, and Mary Magdalene, and some of the disciples might be yonder in the crowd; but they could not come to him, and he could not go to them. It was the hour when he had reached the final depths of suffering. He began to recite the psalm that begins "My God, my God, why hast thou forsaken me?"

But again, as during his agony of prayer in the Garden of Gethsemane, Jesus knew that he could trust his Father's purpose, which, no matter what the darkness, would lead at last to light. He had been faithful to the end, and so he could say now, "It is finished"; and "Father, into thy hands I commit my spirit!"

Then he bowed his head, and breathed his last.

The centurion whose business it had been to carry out the crucifixion stood looking up at Jesus. He had seen many men die, and he was hardened to it. But not to this. "Truly," he exclaimed, "this man was a son of God."

There was a rich man named Joseph of Arimathea who had admired Jesus, but had never been bold enough to be one of his known disciples. He went now to Pilate and asked that he might be allowed to have the body of Jesus and to bury it in a tomb that belonged to him. Pilate gave him permission. So he and some of the women who had loved Jesus took the body down and wrapped it in linen; then they laid it in Joseph's new tomb that had been hewn out of rock, and a great stone was rolled across the entrance.

Now it seemed that everything was over. What had happened to all the bright hopes that had begun that day by the

Lake of Galilee when Jesus said to the first disciples, "Follow me"? What had become of the Kingdom of God that they had thought would come with power on the earth? What power could the disciples see except that which belonged to hate and evil? They had been sure that Jesus, their Master, was the Christ; and now he was dead, and his body laid in Joseph's tomb.

CHAPTER TWENTY-FIVE

Jesus Risen

SOMEWHERE in Jerusalem the disciples were hiding. Their Lord was gone, and now there was nothing to hold them together any longer.

Friday, the day of the crucifixion, died into the night. Saturday, the Jewish Sabbath, came and went. Early the next morning, "the first day of the week," Mary Magdalene and two of the other women who had loved Jesus stole out through the empty streets to go to Joseph of Arimathea's tomb. They brought spices which they meant to lay about the body of Jesus.

The sun was just appearing at the rim of the eastern sky as they drew near the tomb. But even though the light had come, what could they do? They remembered now that a great stone had been placed across the entrance. How could they roll it away?

They came nearer. Then, as they looked, they saw to their amazement that the stone was gone. A figure was there, like a

young man in a white robe; and he said to them: "Do not be
amazed; you seek Jesus of Nazareth who was crucified. He has
risen, he is not here!"

For a moment they stood there trembling. Then with a cry
of joy and wonder they began to run back into the city to
where some of the disciples were. They burst in upon them
with their breathless news—of how they had found the tomb

open and empty, and that they had seen an angel, and that
Jesus was no longer there among the dead.

Peter cried out that he would go and see, and John said he
would go with him. So they ran together. John, being younger,
outran Peter and came first to the tomb. He stopped at the
entrance, not daring to go in. Peter pushed by him, and he
saw the linen that had been wrapped around the body of Jesus

still lying there. Then John followed him, and looked at what Peter had already seen.

But where was Jesus? Was it really true that he had risen?

Or was what had seemed to happen in the morning only some sort of dream, too wonderful to be believed?

Later that day Mary Magdalene came back to the empty tomb, and she was weeping. As she looked up, she saw someone standing near her, who asked her, "Why are you weeping?" She thought it was a gardener, and she said to him, "Sir, if you have carried him away, tell me where you have laid him, and I will take him away."

But the figure simply said to her, "Mary."

That voice! She knew that voice! It was Jesus. She threw herself down at his feet and tried to grasp him. But he told her not to touch him then. She was to find the disciples and tell them that he was going back to God. So she hurried to where they were, and she told them, "I have seen the Lord!"

That evening, according to the Gospel of Luke, two disciples were going out of Jerusalem, home to the little village of Emmaus where they lived. One of them was named Cleophas; the name of the other the Gospel does not tell. They had heard the thrilling news that Jesus was risen; but they had not seen him, and they hardly dared believe it could be true. They were still thinking of the crucifixion, and they were sad.

As they walked along the road, and the shadows of night began to fall, someone whom they did not recognize appeared and joined them. He asked them why they looked so sad. Cleophas asked him if he hadn't heard of what had happened in Jerusalem. He said that they had hoped that Jesus would redeem Jerusalem, but that the chief priests and rulers had condemned him and that he had been put to death.

Then the one who walked at their side asked them why

they were so slow to believe all that the prophets had said. Hadn't they read how it had been foretold that Christ must suffer before he entered into his glory? And then he explained to them what had been written in the Scriptures.

They came to Emmaus, and he looked as though he would leave them and go on. But they begged him not to. "Stay with us," they said, "for it is evening, and the day is now far spent."

So he went with them to their house. They sat down to supper together; and he took the bread and blessed, and broke it, and handed it to them. Suddenly it was as if their eyes had been blind before, and now were opened. As they looked at his face and hands they recognized him. It was Jesus!

Then in a moment he was gone.

They looked at one another and wondered why they had not known him on the road. "Didn't our hearts burn within us," they said, "while he talked to us on the road, and helped us to understand the Scriptures?"

Quickly they rose and hurried back to Jerusalem, where they found the disciples gathered together. They related what had happened in Emmaus, and the disciples told them that Jesus had appeared to Peter, too. Then, before they had finished speaking, they looked up and there in their midst, showing them his hands and feet pierced by the nails of the cross, was Jesus!

On that day Thomas had not been with the rest of the disciples. When they told him that they had seen the Lord, he would not believe it. Then, eight days later—according to the Gospel of John—Jesus came again, and this time Thomas was there. "Do not be faithless, but believing," said Jesus. "Put your finger here—see my hands. Now place your hand here, on my side." It was the place where the spear of one of the soldiers had pierced him while he was on the cross. And

Thomas, no longer doubting, cried out: "My Lord and my God!"

That was in Jerusalem; but the place where Jesus had been most with his disciples was Galilee. It would be natural for some of them to go back there, and according to the Gospel of John they did—to the lake they knew so well, and to the fishing boats they had left. One day they had been fishing before daybreak, and at breakfast time they drew in toward the shore. Someone was standing there. "Who is it?" they asked one another; and one of them whispered, "It is the Lord!"

When Peter heard this, he flung his fisherman's coat about him—for he had been stripped for work—and plunged into the water while the others followed in the boat. When they got to shore, they were too awed to ask if it was Jesus, but they were sure that it was he. And he told them that they would have breakfast there together.

Afterwards Jesus said to Peter, "Do you love me?" Peter answered "Yes, Lord, you know I love you." Again Jesus asked the same question, and also a third time. Peter was distressed that Jesus should repeat his question, and he cried out, "Lord, you know everything; you know I love you!" Well then, from this time on let Peter become the kind of man who could protect those who might be weaker even than he who had denied his Lord. "Feed my sheep," said Jesus, "Feed my lambs."

But if the disciples went back for a while to Galilee, they were not to stay there. It was to Jerusalem that they must go to preach about their Lord. And it was near Jerusalem that he appeared to them once more. According to the Book of the Acts of the Apostles, which was written by the same Luke who wrote the Gospel that bears his name, Jesus had taken them with him one day as far as Bethany. That day he vanished from them to go back to heaven, but not before he had spoken

So Jesus came out, wearing the crown of thorns and the purple robe. Pilate said to them, "Shall I crucify your king?"

"Truly this man was a Son of God!"

He took bread and broke it—and they recognized him.

They cast Stephen out of the city and stoned him; and the witnesses flung down their coats at the feet of a young man named Saul.

these words that they were never to forget. "You shall receive power when the Holy Spirit has come upon you; and you shall be my witnesses in Jerusalem and in all Judea and Samaria and to the end of the earth."

CHAPTER TWENTY-SIX

The Coming of the Holy Spirit

WHEN the risen Lord appeared to the disciples, they were so filled with glad amazement that they could not put all the wonder of it into words. Therefore as we read the Gospels we never get a picture that is clear in every aspect. We cannot know exactly how the risen Jesus looked, nor exactly when and where he came. But the one thing clear beyond all question is that the disciples were sure their Master was alive again. He had made himself known to them with a certainty by which all their minds and hearts were satisfied. And because he was alive, they who had been sunk in despair could begin to live again.

In Jerusalem the disciples began to meet together, to remember Jesus and to pray. Mary, the mother of Jesus, and his brothers were also there.

One had gone now from the twelve men who had been Jesus' closest followers. That one was Judas. When he turned against his Master and made the bargain with Caiaphas and the priests, he was perhaps thinking that, at worst, Jesus would be arrested. When instead, Jesus was not only arrested but condemned to death and crucified, Judas was filled with horror at what he had done. He went back to the priests and cried out that he had betrayed the innocent, and he flung down the money he had been paid. Caiaphas dismissed him with contempt, and in his despair Judas went out and hanged himself.

It seemed to the disciples that someone else should be chosen to make up the number of the twelve. There were two men they thought of, one named Joseph Barsabbas and the other named Matthias; and after they had prayed, they chose Matthias.

On the day of Pentecost, which was one of the great festivals of the Jewish year, they all met together in an upper room —perhaps the same room where they had met on Passover night with Jesus. As they thought of him and prayed together, some immense new power filled the room, strong as a rushing wind, bright as flames of fire. It was the Holy Spirit that Jesus had promised would be given them.

Peter went out and began to preach to the crowds who had come from many lands and who were gathered in Jerusalem. He told of Jesus, and of how the sins of men had crucified him, and of how God had raised him from the dead. "What shall we do?" the people cried. Peter told them that they should be baptized in the name of Jesus, asking forgiveness for their sins, and believing in Jesus who had come as the Christ to save them.

Many were baptized that day. They gathered around the disciples to be taught more about Jesus, to sit down together at the Lord's Supper which he had told them to keep, and to pray that his Spirit would be in their midst again. All of them were Jews, and they still went to the worship in the Temple, as faithful Jews had always done. But they had their own gatherings in someone's house, not on the Jewish sabbath, but on "the first day of the week," because it was that day, Sunday, on which Jesus had risen from the dead.

A new name began to be used for the twelve. They had formerly been called disciples, which meant learners. Now they were called apostles, which meant men who were sent. They were the special witnesses for their Lord. And they were the ones round whom the new believers rallied. These new believers not only worshipped together, but were ready to help one another with everything they had. They brought their possessions to the apostles to distribute among the poor.

Most of them did this gladly; yet here and there were some who wanted to get the credit of giving generously, while secretly they were holding back what they pretended to give. So in the Book of the Acts of the Apostles there is one sad chapter telling of a man named Ananias, and Sapphira his wife, who lied about what they were giving, and who, when they were found out, were so ashamed and shocked that they fell down dead.

Among the apostles, Peter and John were the ones who took the lead. One day they were going up to the Temple at the hour of prayer. There was a man who had been lame from his birth, and whose friends every day would carry him out to one of the Temple gates. He was sitting there begging as Peter and John came by.

He looked up at them, hoping they would drop something in his hand. Peter said he had no money; but he said, "I will give you what I do have: in the name of Jesus Christ of Nazareth, walk!"

He took the lame man by the hand and lifted him up, and suddenly the man felt strength coming into his ankles and his feet. He rose up and began to walk, and went on into the Temple, leaping and praising God.

The astonished people began to flock about, and Peter spoke to them. He said it was not any power and not any goodness

of his or of John's that had made the lame man walk. The
power had come, he said, through Jesus. "His name has made
this man strong. The faith which is come through Jesus has
given him perfect health in the presence of you all."

The report of what had happened spread quickly. It came
to the captain of the Temple and to the Council of the priests.
They were angry to hear that in the Temple itself men were
daring to preach in the name of Jesus—this Jesus whom they
had crucified, and whom they thought they had got rid of
once and for all. Thereupon they had Peter and John arrested,
and shut up in jail until the next day.

In the morning they had Peter and John brought before
them. Caiaphas was there; and so was his father-in-law, old
Annas, who had been high priest before Caiaphas. By what
authority or right, they wanted to know, had Peter and John
presumed to do what they had done?

Peter answered boldly. His authority and power were in the
name of Jesus—the Jesus they had crucified. "This is the stone

which was rejected by you builders," he said, "but which has become the cornerstone." And Peter went on to declare in the face of these rulers, who acted as though they knew all about religion, that only in the name of Jesus Christ could they be saved.

"Who are these uneducated, common men," the members of the Council asked indignantly, "that they should dare speak this way to us?" They recognized these men as having been with Jesus, and this made them all the more resentful. Yet there in front of them was the lame man who had been healed. It was not easy, in the face of the people, to say anything against such healing.

The priests conferred among themselves. They could not deny what had happened, since everyone had seen it. Nevertheless they had no intention of letting this sort of excitement continue. So they forbade Peter and John to speak or teach again in the name of Jesus.

But Peter and John were changed now from the kind of men they had been that night when they had fled in panic from the Garden of Gethsemane. Peter answered that the priests could make up their own minds whether the Council should be listened to, or God; but as for himself and John, they would keep on telling what they knew concerning Jesus.

CHAPTER TWENTY-SEVEN

In the Face of Persecution

THE COUNCIL let Peter and John go, since in the eyes of the crowd they did not have reason enough to punish them. The two then went back to where the other disciples and their friends were met, and there was great rejoicing. They prayed together—not for safety, but for boldness to preach the word of God.

Peter, especially, did keep on preaching. He had a great new power now through his faith in his risen Lord. Sick people were healed when he came where they were. Meanwhile, more and more people were joining the company of the disciples.

Peter, along with some others, was arrested a second time, and put into the common prison, but the next thing the authorities heard was that he had got out and was preaching again in the Temple. Once more, the high priest sent officers to seize Peter and the others and to bring them before the Council, where they were angrily denounced. But this time, there was division in the Council itself. One of the most learned and respected men, Gamaliel, a teacher of the law, stood up and warned the high priest and the rest of the Council against being too rash. He reminded them that when false leaders had arisen among the people their leadership had come to nothing, because it was false. As for these men who were on trial now, the wisest course would be to wait and see. "Let them alone," Gamaliel said. "For if this plan or this undertaking is of men, it will fail; but if it is of God, you will not be able to overthrow it. You might even find yourselves opposing God."

Grudgingly, the rest of the Council took his advice. They called in the apostles and had them beaten. Then they let them go. And in the Book of Acts it is recorded that when they left the presence of the Council, they rejoiced that they were counted worthy to suffer dishonor for the name of Jesus. And every day in the Temple, and wherever people gathered, they were teaching and preaching Jesus as the Christ.

Here and there in Jerusalem, even among the ruling Council, were thoughtful men like Gamaliel. But there were far more who were moved by their own hostile ideas and growing hatreds. That was true of the high priest, Caiaphas, and of all those on the ruling Council who listened to him. Also there was an increasingly ugly temper among many in the Jerusalem crowds. Although great numbers of people had responded to Peter's preaching, others were being stirred up against whatever the disciples said or did. The traders in the Temple had not forgotten how they had been driven out by Jesus, and they spread the word that this Jesus and his followers would destroy the beliefs and the ways of worship that belonged to genuinely faithful Jews.

The hour of peril and of persecution for the disciples had arrived.

There was a young man named Stephen who had been chosen by the disciples as one of seven set apart for special ministry in the care of the poor. Stephen preached with eagerness and power, as though his lips had been touched by the Holy Spirit. But some who heard him one day went and told the priests that he had been speaking blasphemy. So Stephen was arrested and brought before the Council, as Peter and John had been.

Courageously, Stephen did not say what Caiaphas and those who agreed with Caiaphas wanted to hear. Instead, he laid

bare the long record of how often God had sent his messengers
to his people to call them to repentance and of how those messengers had so often been rejected. And now these men to
whom he spoke had at last committed the most dreadful
wickedness of all. He said they had betrayed and murdered
the Righteous One.

When the members of the Council heard that, they ground
their teeth with rage. And when Stephen lifted his face and
cried, "Behold, I see the heavens opened, and the Son of Man
standing at the right hand of God," they stopped their ears
that they might not hear him. The Council turned Stephen
over to a mob that took him outside the walls of the city.
There, they stoned him to death as he prayed, "Lord Jesus,
receive my spirit."

In the crowd that day, not as one of those who were stoning
Stephen, but so close to them that they flung down their coats
at his feet, was another young man, whose name was Saul. He
seemed as far as anyone could be from being a follower of
Jesus, but something began that day which would develop beyond what Saul or anyone else could possibly foresee.

CHAPTER TWENTY-EIGHT

The Conversion
of the Persecutor

AFTER the killing of Stephen, the persecution spread. All who were known to be followers of Jesus were in danger. Many fled from Jerusalem to places that seemed to be more safe. But agents of Caiaphas and the Council were sent after them to track them down and bring them back for trial. Among these agents of the Council was Saul, who had stood by when Stephen was stoned.

Saul of Tarsus he was called, because he came from Tarsus, then an important city in Asia Minor with its harbor on the Mediterranean Sea. Through his family he had the honor of being a Roman citizen, but it was a matter of far greater pride to him that he had been born a Jew. With passionate devotion to history as it was written in the Scriptures, Saul thought of his Jewish race as God's Chosen People, and of Jewish faith and worship as fixed by the unchanging word of God.

Saul had come to Jerusalem to study in the schools of Jewish law. There he had begun to hear of Jesus of Nazareth, who was causing such excitement among the people in Galilee. All he knew about Jesus was that he had been accused of being careless about the law. To Saul's mind that was bad enough; but then the unforgivable had happened. Jesus, with a few disciples of whom no one of importance had ever heard, had

come to Jerusalem at the time of Passover. Jesus had denied
the lawful authorities. He had made a disturbance in the Temple, and—as a crowning blasphemy—he had stood before the
high priest and claimed that he himself was the Messiah foretold by the prophets to come in the name of God. For that
blasphemy he had been rightly condemned and crucified. But
here were these disciples of his who kept up the mad claim
that he was the Christ, and were misleading people by their
preaching. It was all an insult to faithful Jews, and such guilty
people must be got rid of.

So it seemed to Saul of Tarsus; and therefore he went to the
high priest and asked for letters giving him authority to search
for disciples of Jesus, and when he found them to arrest them.
He had heard that some of them had gone as far as the city of
Damascus. He would pursue them there.

One day, then, he set out with an escort on the road that
led north to Damascus. It would be a journey of several days.
It seemed that only one idea was uppermost in Saul's mind—
the fierce purpose to lay hold of these people who had believed
in Jesus and to make sure that they were punished. But was
something else happening in his deeper thoughts? Was he
haunted by a memory he could not push away—the memory
of Stephen, of whom it was said "his face was like the face of
an angel," and who, as he was dying had cried, "Lord Jesus,
receive my spirit"? Was he remembering also the men and
women already arrested in Jerusalem, whose joy and courage
he could not understand? Was he as sure of himself as he had
thought he was?

As to these questions, no one can say; but what later happened is certain, for more than once afterwards Saul told of
it himself.

When he and those who escorted him had almost reached
Damascus, suddenly there was a blaze of light about him. Saul
fell to the ground as though before a stroke of lightning. Then

he heard a voice calling his name. "Saul, Saul," it said, "Why are you persecuting me?"

"Who are you, Lord?" he gasped.

And the answer came, "I am Jesus, whom you are persecuting."

The light that had flamed above Saul had so blinded his eyes that he could not see his way, and the men who were with him took him by the hand and led him into Damascus. In the city there was a disciple named Ananias, to whom word had come, as from God, that he was to go and find Saul and lay his hands on him in healing.

Ananias was dismayed. He knew about this Saul—how much evil he had done already in Jerusalem, and how he had come to Damascus for the very purpose of arrests and persecution. Nevertheless, he was told to go. So Ananias went to the house to which Saul had been brought, and told Saul that he had been sent by the Lord Jesus to pray that Saul might be given back his sight, and that he might be filled with the Holy Spirit. Then it was as though scales fell from Saul's eyes, and he could see. He was baptized; and not only that, he began at once to go into the synagogue at Damascus and to preach Jesus as the Son of God.

Those who heard him were amazed, and they had good right to be. They said that here was the man who had been the enemy of everything that had to do with Jesus. Some, like Ananias, rejoiced. But many in Damascus who sided with the ruling Council in Jerusalem were indignant. They plotted as to how they could kill Saul, and they watched the city gates so that he should not escape. And, in fact, Saul might not have escaped, had not some of the disciples in Damascus made a sling of ropes and in the dark of night let him down outside the walls.

Now this same man who had started out from Jerusalem to Damascus in order to arrest any followers of Jesus whom he

might find went back to Jerusalem, but this time he went
straight to the disciples that he might join himself with them.
But they were afraid of him, and did not believe that he really
meant to be a disciple. How did they know but that he had
come there falsely to get inside their group and then betray
them all? Yet one man had trust enough in Saul to stand up
and be his sponsor. That man was Barnabas, of whom it was
said that he was "a good man, full of the Holy Spirit, and of
faith." Barnabas told how Saul had seen his vision and heard
the voice that spoke to him on the Damascus road. It was true
that Saul had been an enemy of everything that had to do with
Jesus, but in the instant of his vision he had been changed. So
Barnabas dared to believe and to say. And Barnabas was right.
For from the day of his conversion to the end of his life, Saul,
who had been the persecutor, now taking the new name of
Paul, would be the adoring servant of Jesus who had been
revealed to him as the living Lord.

CHAPTER TWENTY-NINE

The Gospel Reaches the Gentiles

A T THE TIME of the conversion of Saul of Tarsus and the beginning of his new ministry, the number of the disciples was being increased in other ways.

One day a disciple named Philip was going along the road that led south from Jerusalem toward the city of Gaza. Behind him came the sound of horses' hoofs and the rolling of chariot wheels and, as Philip looked back at the oncoming chariot, he saw in it an officer of the queen of Ethiopia.

This officer was one of those scattered in many countries who either had been born a Jew or had been won to the Jewish faith. This particular man had even been to Jerusalem to worship. With the horses at a walk and the chariot moving slowly, the Ethiopian held in his hands a copy of the Scriptures, and was reading from the Book of the prophecy of Isaiah. Philip drew near and recognized the words that the Ethiopian was repeating half aloud.

> "As a sheep led to the slaughter
> or a lamb before its shearer is dumb,
> so he opens not his mouth.
> In his humiliation justice was denied him. . . .
> for his life is taken up from the earth.

"Do you understand what you are reading?" Philip asked.

The Ethiopian officer shook his head. No, he did not know what the words meant. He needed someone to interpret them. If Philip knew, let him come up in the chariot and ride with him.

So Philip did; and, as they read the words of the prophet together, Philip began to tell the Ethiopian officer of Jesus. He it was, said Philip, who had laid down his own life that others might be saved. And as he told of the crucifixion and the good news of the risen Jesus, the officer's heart was touched. Close to the road there was a stream. "Look, here is water," said the Ethiopian. "Why should I not be baptized?" He had the chariot brought to a stop, he and Philip went into the stream, and Philip baptized him there.

There was another baptism, too, that was an important sign of how the company of the disciples was widening. This time it marked the conversion of a Roman; and it followed a vision which came to the apostle Peter.

Peter was staying in the city of Joppa, and he had gone up on the flat roof of the house to pray. Before this, all the disciples had come from among the Jews; and many had supposed that it was only to them, the Chosen People, that the Messiah would bring salvation. All the other peoples were Gentiles, with no claim upon the promises of God.

But on this day, as Peter prayed, there came to him a sudden revelation. It was as though a great sheet were let down from the sky with all sorts of birds and animals in it—some of which were of the kinds that teachers of the Jewish law forbade any proper Jew to touch. Peter heard a voice that commanded him to feed on what he saw. "No!" he protested. "I have never eaten anything that is common or unclean." Then the voice replied, "What God has cleansed, you must not call common."

For a moment Peter was bewildered. But almost immediately there came a message that made him understand the meaning of what he had seen and heard. Down at the front door there was a knocking. Three men were there, asking if this was where a man named Simon Peter lodged.

Peter went down to the door and said, "I am the one you are looking for." It was a soldier, together with two servants who stood there, and Peter asked them why they had come. They said that they had been sent from the city of Caesarea by a centurion named Cornelius, a good man who prayed constantly to God. Cornelius, they said, had had an answer to his prayers, and the answer was that he should send for Simon Peter.

Peter invited them in, and the next day he set out with them for Caesarea. When he arrived at the house of Cornelius, he found that the centurion had brought together his kinsmen and his close friends. Peter reminded Cornelius of what he, Peter, had always believed and of what the Roman knew well —that it was unlawful for a Jew to visit or to associate with a Gentile. But he said, "God has shown me that I should not call any man common or unclean. So when I was sent for, I came without objection. I ask then why you sent for me."

Then Cornelius told Peter that four days before there had come to him in his prayers a word from God that he should send for Peter. "So I sent to you at once," he said, "and you have been kind enough to come. Now therefore we are all here present in the sight of God to hear all that you have been commanded by the Lord."

"Truly I perceive," said Peter, "that God shows no partiality, but in every nation any one who fears him and does what is right is acceptable to him." Then Peter went on to tell of Jesus, of his life and death and his rising again, and of how he could bring to all men forgiveness for their sins. The hearts of all those in Cornelius' house who listened to Peter were moved as by the Holy Spirit; and when Peter saw that, he baptized them all.

After the baptism of Cornelius, Peter came back to Jerusalem. He found that some were surprised and troubled at what he had done. Their idea was that the message of salvation was not meant for Gentiles. But Peter recited the whole story of the vision which had come to him in Joppa, of the coming of the messengers from Cornelius, and of what had happened to all those who were gathered in Cornelius' house. "If God gave the same gift to them as he gave to us when we believed in the Lord Jesus Christ," he said, "who was I that I could withstand God?" When they heard that, none of the disciples had anything more to say against it, and they praised God that now the gospel could be preached to men of every race.

Peter had baptized the Roman centurion, Cornelius, a man who was outside the promise that had been assumed to belong only to the people of Israel. But that was not all. The time had come when the gospel should be preached not only in Palestine, but throughout many lands of the wide Roman empire.

In the persecution that had followed the killing of Stephen, some of the disciples were scattered as far away as the city of Antioch—near the corner of the Mediterranean Sea beyond which the long shoreline of Asia Minor reaches toward the west. Antioch was one of the great cities of the Roman world, magnificent with its wide streets, its marble temples, its statues and its fountains. In its crowded population the little company of the followers of Jesus seemed too insignificant for much notice.

It was in Antioch that they were first called "Christians," and the name may have been given them in derision. *Christ-ians!* People who believed that a man who had been crucified was the Christ. To most of the crowd in Antioch that seemed ridiculous. But the little group of disciples who believed in their crucified Lord were about to let loose a power that would go on spreading long after Antioch would be forgotten.

CHAPTER THIRTY

Paul and Barnabas on a Hazardous Journey

THE APOSTLES in Jerusalem had heard of the little church in Antioch and they sent Barnabas there. People who knew Barnabas called him "Son of encouragement," and it was encouragement that he brought to Antioch when he preached. As more people were added to the company of Christians,

Barnabas' ideas were reaching far beyond Antioch. He remembered the man who had been Saul the persecutor, and whom he had introduced to the apostles in Jerusalem as the converted man who took the name of Paul. Paul was in Tarsus, the city from which he had first come. Barnabas went to Tarsus to find him, and he persuaded Paul to come with him to Antioch.

Shortly after that, the church at Antioch was inspired to make a great decision. Instead of keeping Barnabas and Paul there among themselves, these disciples thought of all the people who had never heard of Christ, and to whom Barnabas and Saul could bring the gospel. So they laid hands on these two in blessing, and sent them out as the first Christian missionaries to the lands beyond.

Barnabas and Paul set forth from the seaport of Seleucia and sailed for the island of Cyprus. They took with them a young man named John Mark, who was a cousin of Barnabas. But when they had gone across Cyprus, and into what might be dangerous country on the coast of Asia Minor, John Mark had had enough. He left them, and made his way back to Jerusalem.

Barnabas and Paul continued on their way to the cities inland. The first was Antioch in the providence of Pisidia, not the great Antioch in Syria from which they had started out, but a smaller city of the same name. On a Sabbath Day they went into the synagogue at the hour of regular service, and after the reading from the law and the prophets, the leader of the service turned to the two visitors and asked them whether they had anything to say to the congregation.

Then Paul rose and began to speak. "Men of Israel, and you that fear God, listen," he said. He reviewed the long record of God's dealing with his people: the deliverance from slavery in Egypt, the kingship of David, the promise that some day there should be born of David's line a Savior, the preaching of John the Baptist that the Savior was at hand, and then the coming of Jesus. Paul went on to tell of how the rulers had rejected Jesus and brought him to Pilate to be condemned, and of how he had been crucified and buried, and on the third day had risen from the dead. And now, through him, men could find forgiveness for their sins.

Many in the congregation were moved by Paul's preaching, and the next Sabbath Day a crowd that looked as though it were the whole city was gathered to hear him preach again.

But in the days between, something else had happened. Great numbers of the strict Jews were outraged, just as Caiaphas and the Council in Jerusalem had been. They were not going to admit that there could be any new message from God that would be more important than the laws of Moses. And they took it as an insult to the hopes of Israel that this Paul should preach that one who had been crucified was the promised Christ.

So in the synagogue on this next Sabbath they contradicted Paul and began to shout abuse.

Then Paul and Barnabas made a bold decision. Up to that time they had always preached in the synagogues, because they felt it was there, among the worshiping Jews, that their gospel ought best to be understood. But now they said they would go to all the people, whoever they might be. They would make the gospel "a light for the Gentiles, to bring salvation to the uttermost parts of the earth."

When the fanatics among the Jews heard of this plan, they stirred up a riot against Paul and Barnabas, and drove them out of Antioch. The two apostles then went on to the next city, Iconium, and there the same things happened. Many listened gladly, but others stirred up violence; and Paul and Barnabas were driven out again. But not before they had made new disciples in the name of Jesus, so that in Iconium, as in Antioch also, there was a devoted group who would keep together as a Christian church.

Beyond Iconium, Paul and Barnabas were going into rough country where the people were mostly pagan. Such religion as they had was mostly the old belief that there were many gods who dwelt in the clouds on Mount Olympus; but who, whenever they chose, could take the form of men.

In the city of Lystra Paul came upon a lame man, and he bade him in the name of Jesus to stand up and walk. The man did walk; and when the crowd saw this, they shouted that surely gods had come to earth. Barnabas, they said, must be Zeus, and Paul, the chief speaker, must be Hermes, the messenger of the gods. The priest of the temple of Zeus was about to offer a sacrifice to Paul and Barnabas, and it was all that these two could do to stop him. They were not gods themselves, they explained, but they did bring a message from the living God who had made the heaven and the earth. The apostles would have gone on to preach of Jesus, but the temper of the people turned as sometimes happens in excited crowds. Men had come from Antioch and Iconium with poisonous reports about Paul and Barnabas, and in place of the welcoming tumult there spread now in Lystra the angry menace of an excited mob. These people who a few minutes before had wanted to offer sacrifices to them now laid hold of Paul and Barnabas. Paul especially they stoned, and dragged out of the city, believing him to be dead.

But wounded as he was, Paul was not dead; and he and Barnabas would not be stopped. From Lystra they went on to Derbe, and won many disciples there. Nor did they intend to abandon the disciples they had already made. From Derbe they might have looked for some safe way out. But instead, they went straight back through the cities where they had been assaulted and almost killed; through Lystra and Iconium

and Antioch in Pisidia, strengthening the souls of the disciples, and exhorting them to continue in the faith, and saying that "through many tribulations we must enter the Kingdom of God."

CHAPTER THIRTY-ONE

Paul's Great Adventure in the West

WHEN PAUL and Barnabas returned at length to Antioch in Syria, the city from which they had set out, they gathered the Christians together and told them of all that had happened through the preaching of the gospel in the countries beyond.

The little congregation at Antioch rejoiced, but there were others who were not so pleased with what Paul and Barnabas had done. These were some men from Jerusalem who took offense at the news that the gospel had been preached to Gentiles. They said that unless people submitted to all the laws that had come down from Moses, and were circumcised like all faithful Jews, they could have no part in the promises of God. Paul and Barnabas knew that all their faith in the great meaning of the gospel was on trial now. Had Christ come only to the Jewish people, or did the love of God reach out through him to all the peoples of the earth?

That question needed to be settled. So Paul and Barnabas went to Jerusalem to confer with the apostles there.

When the debate had gone on for a while, Peter stood up. He told again of what had happened to him when the appeal had come from Cornelius, and of how he had gone to Cornelius' house and had baptized there a whole family who were not Jews because the Holy Spirit had come upon them through what they had learned of Jesus.

Everybody listened next to Paul and Barnabas as they told of their work in Asia Minor, and of how the message of the love of God in Jesus had reached the hearts of men who had previously cared little or nothing about God. Then James, one of the brothers of Jesus, summed up what the apostles and the others in Jerusalem thought. It was right, he said, that nothing should be done to discourage the preaching of the gospel to the Gentiles. Let it be understood that the converts should lead clean lives, have nothing to do with the worship of idols, and not hurt the conscience of Jewish fellow Christians by eating what Jews had been trained to regard as unholy food. Beyond that, they would not have to follow the laws and customs that the rabbis and scribes had taught.

All this was put into a letter that was sent back with Paul and Barnabas to Antioch. Now the way was open to carry the gospel far and wide. All peoples, and not the people of Israel alone, could have equal place in the church of Christ.

Paul said to Barnabas, "Come, let us go back and visit the brethren in every city where we proclaimed the word of the Lord, and see how they are getting on." Barnabas was ready. He said they would again take John Mark with them, and that the three of them would start out as they had before. But Paul said no. John Mark had turned back and left them the first time. One failure was enough.

But Barnabas held to his own conviction. John Mark should be given another chance. This was the same Barnabas, "Son of encouragement," who had stood up for Paul when the disciples in Jerusalem knew him only as Saul, the persecutor, and doubted whether his conversion could be real. Now he came to the help of the young John Mark who had failed once, but who—Barnabas believed—would not fail again. Trust him, and he would show that he was worthy to be trusted. So Barnabas said, and he was right, as Paul himself would at length find out. For the time would come when Paul would want John Mark as a companion; and the time would also come when this same Mark, whom Barnabas had stood up for, would help to write one of the Gospels—the Gospel according to Mark.

But Paul could not yet be persuaded, so there was disagreement between him and Barnabas. Barnabas then took Mark and sailed away to preach in Cyprus, while Paul took a disciple named Silas and went back to the cities where he and Barnabas had preached before.

At Lystra, where Paul had been stoned on his first journey, he and Silas found a young man named Timothy, whose mother was a follower of Jesus. Timothy, too, was ready to become a follower, so Paul and Silas took him for a companion, and from that time on Timothy was one of the friends and helpers most dear to Paul.

Through the other cities where Paul had preached before, the three of them journeyed, strengthening the faith of the disciples—across the whole width of Asia Minor, until they came to the city of Troas on the coast of the Aegean Sea. Now they were at the farthest border of the continent of Asia. Beyond them lay the countries and peoples of Europe and the West.

At Troas Paul had a vision. It was as though, across the sea, he saw the lands of Greece, and a young man standing there who called, "Come over to Macedonia and help us!" When Paul had seen that vision, he believed it was the will of God that they should go, so he and Silas and Timothy found a ship on which they could cross over. They had now been joined by another companion, whose name was Luke. He was to be not only a fellow-disciple, but—in Paul's words—"the beloved physician." And it was Luke who afterwards would write the Book of the Acts of the Apostles, and also the Gospel that bears his name.

Across the Aegean Sea they landed at the city of Philippi. By a river bank was a place where a little group of people who believed in God were accustomed to meet for prayer, and Paul and his companions joined them. One of the women, named Lydia, opened her heart to give heed to what Paul preached. She was baptized, together with her family; and she invited Paul and the others to come to her house to stay.

Now, there was a girl in Philippi who went into trances and heard voices as though from beyond this world. Some men who had got hold of her were making money by claiming that she could tell fortunes. When she saw Paul she cried out that Paul and the others with him were servants of God who had come to bring God's message to all the people. Day after day she kept crying after them, as though driven by some wild spirit. But when Paul spoke to her, the wildness vanished and she became quiet again like other people.

Then when the men who had used her for fortune telling saw that they could not make money with her any more, they were furious. Seizing hold of Paul and Silas they dragged them off to a police court. They said that these men, by what they had done to the girl, had taken away their property and had made a disturbance in the city. The Roman magistrate listened to them, and then ordered Paul and Silas to be locked up. Instead of staying in Lydia's house, they would spend the night in prison.

In their cells, Paul and Silas prayed and sang hymns, and the other prisoners listened. The jailer listened too.

Then, about midnight, the city was shaken by an earthquake. The prison rocked on its foundations, and doors were broken open. The jailer was about to kill himself, thinking that all his prisoners would escape and he would be held responsible, but Paul called to him to do nothing rash. When the trembling jailer seized a light and came running in, he found Paul and Silas calm and unafraid in the midst of the broken walls.

The jailer was shaken. "What must I do to be saved?" he cried. "Believe in the Lord Jesus," said Paul, "and you will be saved, you and your household." Then he and Silas told the story of Jesus, and that night the jailer and his family were all baptized.

When it was morning a message came from the Roman magistrates that Paul and Silas were to be released. "The magistrates have sent to let you go," the jailer told them; "now therefore come out and go in peace."

But Paul answered that the magistrates could not end the matter so easily. He was a Roman citizen, and he had been beaten and thrown into jail without a trial. Now should these magistrates only send a message to the jailer? No; let them come themselves. And when the magistrates heard that Paul was a Roman citizen they did come themselves and apologized. Then Paul and Silas went free.

CHAPTER THIRTY-TWO

To Athens and to Corinth

A FTER PAUL and Silas had gone back to Lydia's house and had encouraged the little group of disciples-to-be, they went on to the city of Thessalonica.

In Thessalonica there was a synagogue, and for three weeks at the Sabbath services Paul preached of Jesus. Some of the Jews were persuaded, and a still larger number from among the Greeks who came to listen. But here, as in other cities, were those who thought that Paul's preaching contradicted all that their fathers had believed. What was it but a false message that could preach salvation to Gentiles as well as to Jews?

These men then stirred up some of the tough rabble of the city. Soon a mob gathered and filled the streets with uproar around the house of a man named Jason, where they thought that Paul was staying. When they could not find Paul or Silas, they dragged Jason before the city authorities, crying, "These men who have turned the world upside down have come here also, and Jason has received them; and they are all acting against the decrees of Caesar, saying that there is another king called Jesus!"

Seeing the growing danger, the little group of new disciples in Thessalonica managed to get Paul and Silas away by night. They went to the next city, Beroea, and there again they preached in the synagogue. For a time, they were listened to and welcomed. Then some of the trouble-makers in Thessalonica heard of what was happening, and they came to Beroea and stirred up another riot there.

By ship Paul went on to Athens, while Silas and Timothy remained in Beroea. In Athens Paul met no violence, but rather a cool indifference which blocked him more than violence could have done.

Athens was the most famous center of art and learning in the world. On the crest of a hill, against the deep blue of the Athenian sky, stood the white marble beauty of the Parthenon with its matchless sculptures. Around and below it were other temples that had become the glory of Greece.

In Athens men of great minds and of deep devotion to the truth had lived and taught: Socrates and Plato and Aristotle. But by the time of Paul's arrival it had become the fashion to seem learned. Men of shallow purposes liked to play with ideas, and to match their wits in casual dispute. Some of them decided that they might be amused to find out what this stranger had to say. "What is this new teaching of yours?" they asked him.

Paul began in a way which he thought would capture their attention and their interest. He said that as he had come through Athens he had seen an altar with this inscription: "To an unknown God." This seemed to indicate that they might be reaching up to something or someone greater than they knew. It was this greater message that he, Paul, had come to preach. So he told of the God "in whom we live and move and have our being," and of how this same God of heaven and earth had revealed himself in Jesus, who had lived, been put to death, and then had risen from the dead.

Someone risen from the dead! His listeners laughed at this idea. So that was what this man had to say! They looked at one another and yawned. They said to Paul that perhaps they would hear more from him some other day. A few of the ordinary people in Athens were moved by what Paul preached, but most of those who thought they were learned shrugged him off.

From Athens Paul went on to Corinth. This might have seemed a harder place in which to preach than Athens was. It was a port of call for ships and sailors from all the countries around the Mediterranean Sea—a rough and brawling city that drew to itself not only much of the commerce but many of the vices of the Roman world. Thus, there would not seem to be many inquiring minds in Corinth as there were supposed to be in Athens. But there were in that tough population plenty of human beings who had consciences, and recognized their sins, and might answer to a gospel of salvation.

So Paul settled down in Corinth to earn his living and to take time to reach the people. Month after month he preached, first in the synagogue, and then out among those who knew nothing about religion except to go now and then to a pagan temple.

He did not quote any more from great poets, as he had done in his address in Athens. He was not concerned with tailoring his speech to persons of pretended learning. Instead he determined simply to tell the story by which his own heart had been set on fire—the story of Jesus and of the saving love of God that could lay hold of even the worst of men. "I did not come to you," he wrote afterwards to the Corinthians, "proclaiming to you the testimony of God in lofty words or wisdom. For I decided to know nothing among you except Jesus Christ and him crucified."

That might be a stumbling block to Jews and folly to the Gentiles, but to those who opened their hearts in faith, Christ could become "the power of God and the wisdom of God."

So it turned out in Corinth. The people in that city might not have seemed very promising material. They had plenty of weaknesses and plenty of entanglements with the wickedness around them that would give Paul trouble. But Paul drew the hearts of men and women to become disciples of Jesus, including Crispus, the leader of the synagogue, who was baptized with all his family.

Paul was building a Christian congregation that would live and grow. Meanwhile, he was not forgetting the little groups of new believers whom he had won in the cities of Macedonia, some of whom had suffered persecution as a result. Two letters that he wrote while he was in Corinth are included in the New Testament: the first letter and the second letter to the Thessalonians. "We give thanks to God always for you all," Paul wrote, "constantly mentioning you in our prayers, remembering before our God and Father your work of faith and labor of love and steadfastness of hope in our Lord Jesus Christ. . . . You became imitators of us and of the Lord, for you received the word in much affliction, with joy inspired by the Holy Spirit, so that you became an example to all the believers in Macedonia and in Achaia."

For a considerable time in Corinth there was no violence. Silas and Timothy had come from Macedonia to join Paul. But then there happened what had happened in other cities. Some in the synagogue, possessed by the belief that what Paul preached was destroying obedience to the Jewish laws as they had come down from Moses, began to denounce him. At this point, Paul decided to turn entirely to the Gentiles. This was bound to rouse increasing anger among those most devoted Jews who saw in Paul nothing but a traitor to the faith of Israel. He would be in danger of attack again. But one night in a dream he heard the word of God, "Do not be afraid, for

I am with you." So for a year and a half Paul continued preaching.

Finally, though, his enemies acted. Corinth was governed by the Roman proconsul, Gallio. The Jewish group that hated Paul now seized him and brought him to Gallio's court. "This man is persuading men to worship God contrary to the law," they said. But the Roman dismissed them with contempt. If Paul had been accused of some vicious crime, Gallio said, that would have been something for him to take account of. But as for disputes about words and names and matters of their own law, they could look after it themselves. He would not bother himself about their differences. So Gallio drove the accusers out from his tribunal, and paid no attention when the crowd outside took the leader of the synagogue group and beat him.

This time a Roman official had protected a Christian preacher. But not with any genuine understanding. To Gallio, what Paul was preaching seemed only some notion that did not matter. He could not know that in it was a power that would be more important than all the power of Rome.

Paul stayed a while longer in Corinth, then took passage on a ship to sail back across the Aegean Sea. Two new converts went with him, Aquila and Priscilla his wife. They came to the great city of Ephesus on the coast of Asia Minor. As so often in other places he went first to the synagogue, and many in the congregation wanted him to stay. Paul said no, but that if God willed it, he would come again. Then he embarked on the long voyage back to Palestine; and, landing at Caesarea, he went up to Antioch. For the second time he was bringing to the church there his report on the preaching of the gospel in the far countries to which he had been sent.

CHAPTER THIRTY-THREE

Perilous Doors of Opportunity

For PAUL there was no long tarrying, even in Antioch. He had hardly arrived before he was starting out again. He had not forgotten his promise to come back to Ephesus.

Once more he went through the cities in Asia Minor, bringing encouragement to the little congregations of Christians which his first preaching had gathered there. Then, by long overland journeys, he came to Ephesus.

There had been some preparation already for the preaching of the gospel in that city. Priscilla and Aquila had stayed there when they had come before with Paul, and had remained after he had gone on his way to Palestine. Also, there was a devout Jew named Apollos, who had been moved by the preaching of John the Baptist, and then had heard of Jesus. Priscilla and Aquila had taught him, as well as they could, what they had learned from Paul. Now Apollos had gone back to Greece; but when Paul arrived in Ephesus, he found that many people had been listening to Apollos' preaching there.

Paul discovered that Apollos' message had not gone much beyond the message of John the Baptist. It was a call to repent, before God's punishment came. But Paul had more to proclaim. His preaching centered in Jesus: in the love of Jesus reaching out to all human souls, no matter how sinful they

*As Paul approached Damascus, suddenly a light from heaven
flashed about him.*

Paul and Barnabas set sail on their first mission.

And they brought Paul to the Areopagus, saying, "May we know what this new teaching is?"

Paul on trial before Festus, the Roman governor at Caesarea.

may have been; in Jesus crucified, as the final sign that God's love in him will suffer to the utmost in order that it may save; in Jesus risen from the dead, as the promise that his living Spirit will come to those who take him as their Lord. Now those who had been gathered by Apollos were baptized by Paul in the name of Jesus, and they were glad.

For two years Paul preached and taught in Ephesus, and his preaching had such power that many who had been sick were healed. Other men, who had pretended that they could cure people by magic spells, were converted, and afterwards they brought their books of quack prescriptions and threw them into the fire.

Yet some of these men had what they thought was a smart idea. They would listen to Paul and watch exactly what he said and did. Perhaps he had a magic word, and one which was better than theirs. They listened, and thought they had the secret. So one day, when they happened to meet a poor crazy creature, they said to what they supposed was an evil spirit in him, "We adjure you by the Jesus whom Paul preaches." But the man answered, "Jesus I know, and Paul I know; but who are you?" And the man leaped on them, ripped off their clothes, and drove them off naked and wounded.

Others in Ephesus were still more concerned about the preaching of Paul. In Ephesus was the great temple of the goddess Diana. It was so famous, and so many thousands of people believed in what the goddess might do for them if they brought her gifts, that much of the business of Ephesus depended upon the temple worship. People would buy little silver images of the great statue of the goddess, and the silversmiths who made these images got their living from that trade. Now, because of Paul's preaching, worship of the goddess was growing less.

One of the silversmiths, a man named Demetrius, was

alarmed at this. He called together other makers and sellers of the images. They knew as well as he did, he said, that it was by this business that they got their wealth. If people stopped coming to the temple, that would be an end to their money-making. Moreover, if the temple lost its fame, then Ephesus, which now was known throughout the world, would become only another ordinary city.

His words were like a match dropped into tinder. The men who listened to him were enraged at his picture of what might happen to the temple and to their trade. "Great is Diana of the Ephesians," they shouted, and pouring out into the streets, they filled the city with confusion. They stormed into an amphitheater where they supposed Paul would be speaking, dragging with them Gaius and Aristarchus, companions of Paul whom they had chanced to find.

When Paul knew that the crowd was there, he wanted to go into the midst of it, but the disciples and others who were his friends begged him not to try it. Meanwhile, one of the high officials of the city had come upon the scene. He managed to quiet the mob while he spoke. Everyone knew, he said, that Ephesus was the city of the great goddess Diana, and always would be. Of course everyone wanted to retain the temple and the worship that centered there. But there were lawful and unlawful ways of going about the matter. If they had complaints against anyone, let them bring these to the courts. Right now they were in danger of being charged with rioting, the official said, and of having no sufficient cause to justify the whole commotion. Then he ordered the mob to disperse.

The dangers around Paul did not frighten him. "I have fought with beasts at Ephesus," he wrote in one of his letters; but no matter how much danger there might be from men whose hatred made them act like beasts, he rejoiced in his chance to spread the gospel. "A wide door for effective work

has opened to me," he wrote, "and there are many adversaries."
Note that *and* is what he wrote, not *but*. The dangers and the
difficulties he would have to face did not make the "wide door"
less inviting, but all the more so!

Yet what lay heavy on Paul's heart was the fact that there
were troubles in the church in Corinth. Some of the new converts were slipping back into old sins. Some would-be teachers
had sprung up and were splitting the little church into fac-
tions. So Paul wrote and sent from Ephesus the burning mes-
sages which are included in the New Testament as the First
and Second Letters to the Corinthians—letters full of sorrow
and rebuke and also of exultancy and thanksgiving, depending
on how the Corinthians responded.

It is in one of these letters that Paul recorded what he
had faced and endured as he had carried the gospel across
the Roman world: five times whipped by Jewish mobs, three
times scourged by Roman magistrates, stoned once, three
times shipwrecked. "A night and a day," he wrote, "I have
been adrift at sea; on frequent journeys, in danger from
rivers, danger from robbers, danger from my own people,
danger from Gentiles, danger in the city, danger in the wilderness, danger at sea, danger from false brethren; in toil and
hardship, through many a sleepless night, in hunger and
thirst, often without food, in cold and exposure. And, apart
from other things, there is the daily pressure upon me of my
anxiety for all the churches."

Was he pitying himself for all that? No! "For the sake of
Christ," he wrote, "I am content with weaknesses, insults,
hardships, persecutions and calamities; for when I am weak,
then I am strong." He had heard the promise of Christ. "My
grace is sufficient for you."

In the letters to the Corinthians Paul dealt one by one with
the problems—and sometimes the disputes—that had been
brought to him. And along with his counsel concerning par-

ticular matters of the church, is his setting forth of what he
believed about the supreme aspects of the Christian faith:
about the church, about the celebration of the Lord's Supper,
about the resurrection, about the things that abide—faith,
hope, and love. And notwithstanding all the times when the
Corinthians had disappointed him, he was sure that "the grace
of the Lord Jesus Christ, and the love of God, and the fellow-
ship of the Holy Spirit" would be with them still.

Not long afterward, Paul decided to visit again the Christian
churches that he had founded in Macedonia and Greece. For
about three months he went from city to city, and then came
back across the Aegean Sea to Asia Minor. He wanted to be
in Jerusalem for the celebration of the Passover, and the time
was growing short. So he could not stop in Ephesus; but he
sent a message to the elders of the Ephesian Church and asked
them to come and meet him at the seaport of Miletus.

They did come, and Paul poured out his heart to them. He
reminded them, as they talked together, of all that had happened in Ephesus when he was there. He told them that he
could not know what dangers he might meet now that he was
going to Jerusalem, but he believed these would be great. They
might even mean his death. Let that be as it might. "I do not
account my life of any value nor as precious to myself," he
said, "if only I may accomplish my course and the ministry
which I received from the Lord Jesus, to testify to the gospel
of the grace of God."

Now the important thing was that they should understand
what they themselves must do as guardians of the church. Men
with wrong ideas and selfish purposes would appear, he said,
who would be as dangerous as wolves in a flock of sheep. They,
the elders, must have the same patience and devotion which
they knew that he, Paul, had tried to have in the three years
he had been among them. "Now I commend you to God and
to the word of grace that is able to build you up," he said.

They were to help the weak, and to remember the words of the Lord Jesus when he said, "It is more blessed to give than to receive."

Then he knelt down and prayed with them all. They threw their arms about Paul, and they wept at the thought that they might never see his face again. They took him to his ship—the ship that was to carry him toward perils far worse than they could foresee.

CHAPTER THIRTY-FOUR

The Fury of the Jerusalem Crowd

EASTWARD across the Mediterranean, by one ship and then by another, Paul went on his way. Landing at length at Caesarea, he was met by disciples who begged him not to go to Jerusalem, for they dreaded the arrest and possible violence that might be awaiting him there. But Paul said to them, "What is this that you are doing, weeping as though to break my heart? I am ready not only to be imprisoned, but even to die at Jerusalem for the name of the Lord Jesus."

They knew then that no pleading of theirs could change his purpose; and they said, "The will of the Lord be done."

So Paul went on to Jerusalem, and the next morning he met with all the leaders of the disciples there. He told them of what God had accomplished through him in his preaching of the gospel in all the lands where he had been. James, who presided, and all the others who listened to him, rejoiced. But they knew well enough that there were many in Jerusalem who hated Paul, especially those who kept their fierce devotion to all the Jewish worship and the Jewish law, and who looked upon Paul as a destroyer of what they had been taught to protect.

But the disciples thought that there might be a way by which Jews like those could be shown that there was no real reason for hating Paul. There were four men who had made a vow that could be carried out only by special acts of worship and contributions in the Temple. Would Paul go with them and show thus that he had never ceased to be loyal to the great heritage of Israel?

Yes, Paul would go. And he did go; but the result was not what had been hoped for. Instead of quiet and good will, there was a new outburst of anger. Some of the more fanatical Jews, when they saw Paul in the Temple, got the mistaken idea that he had come there for some insulting purpose. They stirred up a crowd and cried out, "Men of Israel, help! This is the man who is teaching men everywhere against the people and the law and this place: moreover he also brought Greeks into the Temple, and he has defiled this holy place."

The excitement spread into a riot. Men ran together, seized Paul, and dragged him out of the Temple. As they were about to kill him, word of what was happening came to the tribune in command of the Roman troops responsible for keeping order in Jerusalem. This tribune went at once with his centurions and their soldiers, and the crowd, seeing them coming, stopped beating Paul.

The tribune then put Paul under arrest, fastening chains on his wrists. "Who is this man and what has he done?" the tribune demanded. Some of the crowd shouted one thing and some another, so that the tribune could make nothing out of the uproar. "Bring him into the barracks," the tribune ordered; and the yelling crowd pressed in so violently that the soldiers had to pick up Paul and carry him.

At the gate of the barracks, Paul spoke to the tribune. He was surprised that Paul spoke to him in Greek. He somehow had the idea that Paul might be a certain Egyptian rebel for whom the authorities had been looking. But Paul said, "No. I am a Jew from Tarsus in Cilicia. I beg you let me speak to the people."

The tribune gave him leave; and Paul, standing on the barracks steps, made a gesture for silence so commanding that the crowd was hushed. Then he spoke to them in Hebrew.

He told how he had come from Tarsus to Jerusalem to the school of the great Jewish rabbi Gamaliel, to be educated, he said, "according to the strict manner of the law of our fathers, being zealous for God as you all are this day.'

He told them then of how he had persecuted the followers of Jesus, of how he had started on his journey to Damascus to hunt some of them down—and of how on the road he had seen his vision of Jesus and had been converted. He told them also that he had come back then to Jerusalem, and that one day in the Temple he had heard the voice of God saying to him that he was to go out and preach of Jesus as the savior—not only for the Jews but also for the Gentiles.

When the crowd heard that about the Gentiles, there went up a furious shout, "Away with such a fellow from the earth! For he ought not to live."

The tribune, angry and impatient, had had enough of this. He ordered Paul to be brought inside the barracks and to be scourged, since he seemed somehow to be the cause of continuing tumult. But when he had been tied up for the scourging, Paul said to the centurion whom the tribune had put in charge: "Is it lawful for you to scourge a man who is a Roman citizen, and uncondemned?" When the centurion heard this, he realized that he might get into trouble. So he went off to the tribune, and said to him, "What are you about to do? This man is a Roman citizen."

The tribune came and asked Paul, "Are you a Roman citizen? Tell me." Paul answered, "Yes."

"I bought my citizenship for a large sum," the centurion said. "But *I* was born a citizen," Paul replied. Then the tribune was much concerned, as the centurion had been. Wishing to get the whole matter off his own hands if he could, he commanded that Paul should be released from his chains.

The tribune then sent a summons to the chief priests and their Council to meet on the following morning; at that time he brought Paul before them to see if he could find out thus what Paul might be accused of.

Looking intently at the members of the Council Paul began, "Brethren, I have lived before God in all good conscience up to this day—"

Before he could continue, the high priest Ananias commanded those who stood near Paul, "Strike him on the mouth!"

Indignantly Paul answered, "God shall strike you, you whitewashed wall! Are you sitting to judge me according to the law, and yet contrary to the law you order me to be struck?"

Those who stood by demanded, "Would you revile God's high priest?"

"I did not know, brethren, that he was the high priest," Paul answered; and he added, "It is written, 'You shall not speak evil of a ruler of your people.' "

Then Paul paused and looked at the men of the Council. He knew that some of them were Pharisees and some were Sadducees, and he knew also that there could be sharp differences between them. The Sadducees were men who kept the forms of religion but had not as deep a belief in God either for this life or the life beyond as the Pharisees had. So Paul began, "Brethren, I am a Pharisee, a son of Pharisees; with respect to the hope and the resurrection of the dead I am on trial."

Immediately the Council fell into disagreement. Some of the Pharisees' party stood up and said, "We find nothing wrong in this man. What if a spirit or an angel spoke to him?" The Sadducees thought this was nonsense; and the dispute in the Council grew so bitter that there was nothing for the Roman tribune to do but to take Paul back under protective arrest.

There would be need of protection. The next day some of the most fanatical men from the crowd, hating Paul, got together to decide what they could do. There were forty of them, and they bound themselves by an oath not to eat or drink until they had killed Paul. They went to members of the Council who also wanted to get rid of Paul, and this was the plot they hatched: the Council was to ask the tribune to send Paul to them for another hearing. While Paul was being led there, the forty men from an ambush in the street would set upon him and kill him before the Roman guard could bring reinforcements great enough to interfere.

Fortunately, however, the son of Paul's sister happened to be in Jerusalem, heard of the plot, and went and told the tribune.

The tribune at this point determined that whatever was

to be done with Paul should be passed on to higher authority. He then called two of his centurions and told each of them to take two hundred men, together with seventy horsemen, and to escort Paul to Caesarea; there, they were to deliver him to the resident Roman governor.

The tribune also wrote this letter to be delivered with Paul:

Claudius Lysias to his Excellency the governor Felix, greeting. This man was seized by the Jews, and was about to be killed by them, when I came upon them with the soldiers and rescued him, having learned that he was a Roman citizen. And desiring to know the charge on which they accused him, I brought him down to their Council. I found that he was accused about questions of their law, but charged with nothing deserving death or imprisonment. And when it was disclosed to me that there would be a plot against the man, I sent him to you at once, ordering his accusers also to state before you what they have against him.

CHAPTER THIRTY-FIVE

Paul's Defense, and His Appeal to Caesar

PAUL, and the letter concerning him, were delivered by the escort to the governor, Felix, in Caesarea. He asked Paul a few indifferent questions, and then ordered that he should be kept under guard until his accusers should appear.

Five days later, some priests and elders, together with a lawyer named Tertullus, came down from Jerusalem. Addressing the governor and looking at Paul, Tertullus declared: "We have found this man a pestilent fellow, an agitator among all the Jews throughout the world, and a ringleader of the sect of the Nazarenes. He even tried to profane the Temple, but we seized him. By examining him yourself, you will be able to learn from him everything of which we accuse him."

But the governor was not impressed. He listened to Paul as he replied to Tertullus' charges. Then he put the accusers off. He would not decide the case, he said, until Claudius Lysias, the tribune, came down to Caesarea.

Yet there was something about Paul that made the Roman governor uneasy. The wife of the governor was a Jewess, and perhaps through her he had some idea of the judgments of God. He sent for Paul and heard him speak of faith in Jesus Christ. Then he was still more uneasy, but he was not yet ready to do anything about what he had heard. He declared that he would listen to Paul again if he had time. And in fact, he did have other conversations with him later, for he had the secret idea that if he kept Paul long enough he might be offered a bribe to set Paul free. But when two years had gone by, Felix was removed by the emperor from his governorship; and another governor, Porcius Festus, was appointed in his place.

Soon after Festus had arrived in Caesarea he went up to Jerusalem, and the chief priests and the principal men of their party urged him to have Paul brought to Jerusalem for trial—for they thought also that this time it might be possible to have him set upon and killed on the way. But Festus refused. He said he was returning shortly to Caesarea, that Paul was being kept there, and that those who wanted to accuse him could come there and state what they had against him.

Once more, then, the enemies of Paul brought their charges against him, and once more he made his reply: "Neither against the law of the Jews, nor against the Temple, nor against Caesar have I offended at all." Festus asked him whether he would choose to be taken to Jerusalem and tried in a Jewish court. But Paul replied: "I am standing before Caesar's tribunal, where I ought to be tried; to the Jews I have done no wrong, as you know very well. If, then, I am a wrongdoer and have committed anything for which I deserve to die, I do not seek to escape death; but if there is nothing in their charges against me, no one can give me up to them. I appeal to Caesar."

This meant that Paul claimed the right as a Roman citizen to have his case referred to the emperor himself. Festus conferred with his council. Then he announced, "You have appealed to Caesar; to Caesar you shall go."

Some time went by before arrangements could be made to send Paul to Rome. One day, meanwhile, a royal visitor arrived in Caesarea. Herod Agrippa, who was allowed by the Romans to rule as king over one of the provinces of Palestine, came to visit the new governor. Festus conferred with him about Paul. He told Herod how he had found Paul left by Felix as a prisoner and how the Jewish Council had wanted Paul condemned. "But I answered them," said Festus, "that it was not the custom of the Romans to give up any one before the accused met the accusers face to face, and had opportunity to make his defense concerning the charge laid against him." Festus also told Herod how he had held a trial, but could make nothing out of the whole matter. And now Paul had appealed to the emperor.

Agrippa said to Festus, "I should like to hear the man myself," and Festus answered, "You shall hear him tomorrow."

So the next day Herod and his sister, Bernice, were ushered with much pomp into Festus' audience hall, and Paul was brought in.

Festus told Herod that this was the man he had already described to him as having appealed to Caesar. "But I have nothing definite to write my lord about him," Festus said. "I have brought him before you so that, after we have examined him, I may have something to report."

Would Herod, then, take over the prisoner and question him?

Herod said to Paul, "You have permission to speak for yourself."

Then Paul made his defense.

He told of his early life. "According to the strictest party of our religion," he said, "I have lived as a Pharisee." And he went on to tell of how he had persecuted the followers of Jesus, even to distant cities.

"Thus I journeyed to Damascus," he said, "with the authority and commission of the chief priests. At midday, O king, I saw on the way a light from heaven, brighter than the sun, shining round me and those who journeyed with me. And when we had all fallen to the ground, I heard a voice saying to me in the Hebrew language, 'Saul, Saul, why do you persecute me? It hurts you to kick against the goads.' And I said, 'Who are you, Lord?' And the Lord said, 'I am Jesus whom you are persecuting. But rise and stand upon your feet; for I have appeared to you for this purpose, to appoint you to serve and bear witness to the things in which you have seen me and to those in which I will appear to you, delivering you from the people and from the Gentiles. To whom I send you to open their eyes, that they may turn from darkness to light and from the power of Satan to God, that they may receive forgiveness of sins and a place among those who are consecrated by faith in me.' "

The glory of what he was remembering burned now in Paul like an increasing flame, and his voice rang out as he exclaimed "Wherefore, O King Agrippa, I was not disobedient to the heavenly vision! I declared first to those at Damascus, then at Jerusalem, and throughout all the country of Judea, and also to the Gentiles, that they should repent and turn to God and perform deeds worthy of their repentance."

He also told them how some among the Jews had tried to kill him because he had gone out to show that it was not only the Chosen People who belonged to God. Nevertheless, what he preached, he said, was "what the prophets and Moses had said would come to pass: that the Christ must suffer, and that by being the first to rise from the dead, he would proclaim light both to the people and to the Gentiles."

Then for the first time the silence in the listening hall was broken. It was the voice of the governor that spoke. "Paul, you are mad!" said Festus.

But Paul answered that he was not mad, and that what he spoke was sober truth. And turning from the Roman to the Jew he said, "King Agrippa, do you believe the prophets? I know that you do believe."

But Herod Agrippa rebuffed him with a sneer. "In a little while you will be trying to make *me* into a Christian," he said.

"I would to God that not only you but also all who hear me this day might become such as I am—except for these chains," Paul answered.

With that, the king and the governor and those who had been sitting with them rose. And when they had left the hall, the governor and the king said to one another, "This man is doing nothing to deserve death or imprisonment." He might even have been set free, they agreed, if he had not already made his appeal to Rome.

CHAPTER THIRTY-SIX

Paul Finishes His Course

THE TIME had come for Paul to be sent to the emperor for trial, and he was delivered, with some other prisoners, into the charge of a centurion named Julius. Luke and another companion, named Aristarchus, were allowed to go with Paul.

They were put on board a ship which set sail for what would be a long voyage of more than a thousand miles across the Mediterranean Sea to Italy and thence to Rome. Touching first at Sidon on the coast not far from Caesarea, the ship then turned its bow westward past the island of Cyprus, and came into harbor at the city of Myra on the coast of Asia Minor. There the centurion found another ship that he thought would cover the distance to Italy in a shorter time, and transferred his prisoners to that ship. But the winds fell, and the ship made poor progress, and much time had been lost when at length it came in sight of the harbor of Fair Havens, on the southern shore of the island of Crete.

Winter was coming on when the weather would change, and the sea be rough and dangerous. There was discussion as to whether the ship should drop anchor in Fair Havens; but the centurion and the ship's captain determined to run the risk of going further. And at first it seemed that they were right. With a fair wind filling her sails, the ship went on her way.

But suddenly the wind shifted. It went round to the northeast, and blew into a furious gale. The crew did their best to

On the island of Malta, Paul shakes off the deadly viper.

Paul, in prison, writing to the churches he loved.

brace the hull of the ship against the pounding of the seas, and to keep her headed on her course, but hour by hour both wind and water struck with greater violence. Sails that had not been reefed in time were ripped away, the steering gear was no longer manageable, and the whole ship plunged and shud-

dered as though at any moment it might go down. To lighten it, the crew hauled up the cargo and threw it overboard together with all the extra tackle and other heavy things they could get rid of.

For several days and nights the ship plunged blind and helpless before the pursuing storm. Then soundings showed that they were coming into shoal water. Some of the sailors, terrified lest the ship might be dashed to pieces on land in the darkness, tried to lower a boat on the chance of getting ashore. Except for Paul, panic might have spread. He said that in the night he had seen an angel, who had told him that it was God's purpose that he should come safe to Rome. Let the whole ship's company therefore take heart. Not a man among them would be lost.

Dawn came at last. There ahead could be seen a bay with a beach. A foresail was hoisted to get the ship in—in anywhere —from the raging sea. The wind drove the ship headlong toward the shore—until it shocked on a reef underneath, with the bow stuck fast, and the stern being smashed in the pounding of the surf. Some of the soldiers were about to kill the prisoners, but the centurion prevented it. He ordered everyone overboard, first those who could swim, and then those who could get hold of planks or other pieces of the ship as it broke up. Thus the prisoners and the whole crew got to the shore.

It turned out that this land to which Paul and his companions had escaped was the island of Malta. The people of the island did everything they could to help. They built a fire where the shipwrecked men, crawling out of the surf, could come and warm themselves. But some of the superstitious ones among them received a shock. Paul had picked up a bundle of sticks to put on the fire and, suddenly, out of the sticks crawled a viper and fastened itself on his hand. "This is some murderer or other criminal, and now justice has caught up with him," the people thought. But Paul shook the snake off into the fire; and, when the men around him saw this, and saw also that he was not bitten, they changed their minds and said that he must be a god.

With the ship that had brought them to the island wrecked, there was no way of going farther until another ship bound for Italy might appear. Julius, the centurion, liked Paul, and treated him with much consideration. He allowed Paul to stay at the house of Publius, a prominent man of Malta. And Publius, as well as others on the island, had reason to be grateful that Paul was there. When Publius' father was ill,

Paul went in to see him and prayed, and laid his hands on the old man and healed him; and he did the same for others who were sick.

Three months went by before another ship was ready, and then once more Paul and his companions were on the way to Italy. Again it was a slow voyage, but this time a safe one. When the ship made port at the Italian harbor of Puteoli, Christian disciples welcomed Paul. And as he was escorted on the road to Rome, other disciples came to meet him on the Appian way, and went with him into the city. Until his appeal should come up for decision in the imperial court, Paul was kept under constant guard; but he had much freedom to have people come to see him.

There was a large colony of Jews in Rome, and Paul invited the leaders of the synagogue to meet him. Here, as always, his longing turned to those who, like himself, belonged to the lineage of Israel and who shared with him the faith of the Chosen People. He reviewed for them some of the story of his own life, and tried to convince them that, in Jesus, all that Moses and the prophets had looked forward to was fulfilled. Some of them were greatly moved, but others disagreed, all the more so because they saw that Paul would continue to carry his gospel to the Gentiles.

Besides the synagogue, there was already a little Christian congregation in Rome. No one knows how it began. Men and women whose names are long since lost must have been responsible for it—disciples who like The Unknown Soldier are "known only to God"; some coming perhaps from Jerusalem, or from Antioch, and spreading in the great city the message of Jesus that had touched their lives at home.

However it was that the Christian church in Rome had started, it was *there*. Paul had written a letter to this church when he was in Corinth; and that letter, preserved now in the New Testament, is the greatest expression by Paul of what

Christ had meant to him. It must be read and pondered in its entirety if one is to understand the greatness and glory of Paul's faith—that Jesus on his cross had taken upon himself the whole awful weight of the world's sin, and that Jesus risen could lift men with him into victory over sin and to new life here and in the world to come. "Who shall separate us from the love of Christ?" Paul had written. "Shall tribulation, or distress, or persecution, or famine, or nakedness, or peril, or sword? No, in all these things we are more than conquerors through him who loved us. For I am sure that neither death, nor life, nor angels, nor principalities, nor things present, nor things to come, nor powers, nor height, nor depth, nor anything else in all creation will be able to separate us from the love of God in Christ Jesus our Lord."

Paul's case came at length to trial. The charges against him were dismissed, and he was set free. But not for long. He was arrested again. In the Roman empire, Christians were beginning to be regarded with suspicion. This "Kingdom of God" they talked about—was there some conspiracy in that? Were these Christians some secret group of enemies of Rome?

Imprisoned the second time, Paul knew now that his time was short. He could never go again to see the churches he had founded, and the men and women he loved, in Asia Minor, in Macedonia, and in Greece. But he could write letters—letters that now are a part of the New Testament. He wrote to his friend Philemon about an escaped slave Onesimus who was coming back, and who Paul wanted to be treated with gentleness and Christian love. He wrote to Timothy: "Do your best to come to me soon . . . for the time of my departure has come. I have fought the good fight, I have finished the race, I have kept the faith." He wrote to the church at Colosse: "Put on, as God's chosen ones, holy and beloved, compassion, kindness, lowliness, meekness and patience, forbearing one another and, if one has a complaint against another, forgiving each other; as the Lord has forgiven you, so you also must forgive. And above all these, put on love, which binds everything together in perfect harmony. And let the peace of Christ rule in your hearts, to which indeed you were called in the one body, and be thankful."

Also he wrote, to the church that seems to have been nearest to his heart, the letter to the Philippians: "I thank my God, in all my remembrance of you." And he continued: "I want you to know, brethren, that what has happened to me has really served to advance the gospel, so that it has become known throughout the whole praetorian guard, and to all the rest, that my imprisonment is for Christ; and most of the brethren have been made confident in the Lord because of my imprisonment and are much more bold to speak the word of God without fear."

As Paul looked back upon his life, and now as he looked ahead, his one great desire was for such faith in Christ "that I may know him and the power of his resurrection, and may share his sufferings, becoming like him in his death, that if possible I may attain the resurrection from the dead. Not that I have already obtained this or am already perfect; but I press on to make it my own, because Christ Jesus has made me his own."

CHAPTER THIRTY-SEVEN

The Victory of Christ

THE EMPEROR of Rome was Nero, now of evil memory. When he had come to the throne as a young man, influenced by the wise counsellor Seneca, much good was expected of him. He had superficial qualities which made him popular, but he was vain and selfish and of a savage temper.

On the 18th of July in the year 64 A.D., a fire broke out in Rome that spread into a ruinous conflagration. For six days it raged, and when it had burned as far as it could go, great sections of the city had been destroyed. In the panic of the spreading fire, all sorts of rumors ran among the people as to how the fire started. Some said that Nero himself had had it set—Nero, who in his vanity wanted to get rid of the ugly part of Rome and to rebuild it magnificently. But Nero, looking for a scapegoat, accused the Christians. Many of them were seized, tortured, and cruelly killed in the open spaces outside of Nero's palace.

About that same time, Paul was taken from his prison and put to death. He had fulfilled what he had written to the Church in Philippi that it might be God's purpose "that for the sake of Christ" a disciple "should not only believe in him but also suffer for his sake."

From this time on, there were other persecutions of the Christians. The last book in the New Testament is "The Revelation to John." Apparently it was written near the end of the first century during the persecution set afoot by the emperor Domitian. Its purpose was to give courage and strength to those who otherwise might have been in despair. "Be faithful unto death, and I will give you the crown of life," was its message to the churches.

In a series of tremendous visions it prophesied the judgment that should come upon all who tried to destroy the invincible purpose of God in Christ. The pagan power of Rome would be destroyed, and to the Lamb—the symbol of Christ sacrificed on the cross—should be "Blessing and glory and wisdom and thanksgiving and honor and power and might."

It would have been too perilous to the Christians for this book to be read and understood by the persecutors, and so the name of Rome was never used, but "Babylon" instead. Nevertheless the Christians knew what was meant when they read: "Fallen, fallen is Babylon the great . . . for mighty is the Lord God who judges her." And at the end of the book is the vision of a new heaven and a new earth, wherein righteousness shall dwell.

So the New Testament comes to its conclusion, and the first century of the calendar that began with the birth of Jesus was ended. Paul had gone to his martyr's death in Rome. According to the tradition that has come down from the early church, Peter also was executed there. John, the disciple whom Jesus loved most, was said to have lived to old age; and his name is linked with the great Fourth Gospel and its message of Jesus as the Way, the Truth and the Life. Now John also was dead; and James, his brother, the other one who responded to Jesus' call that day at the Lake of Galilee, had been put to death long ago in Jerusalem. These were the brothers who had asked Jesus, "Grant that we may sit one on thy right hand and the other on the left in thy Kingdom."

Where, the scornful persecutors might have asked, is any Kingdom now?

But it had begun, and it has been growing ever since.

It was not to be like the kingdoms of this earth—as Jesus had said to Pilate. It would not be built by force or by compulsion. It would not depend on outward circumstance. It must be built by the Spirit of Jesus, of whom Henrik Ibsen, the dramatist, in one of his plays had the last pagan emperor of Rome say that, while the so-called conquerors vanish, he "sits throned as the King of love in the warm believing hearts of men."

When the apostle Peter stood before the priests and rulers in Jerusalem and proclaimed the risen Christ, he said: "There is no other name given among men by which we may be saved." From that time to this, men and women beyond all counting have known in themselves the truth that Peter knew. When they have wanted to be saved from the things that made them ashamed—saved from their wrongdoings and their weaknesses and their sins, saved from their own worse selves—they have looked at Jesus and seen what life at its highest ought to be. But that is not enough. The perfect example, by itself, could seem too far off to be of help. What human beings need to feel is that the love of God himself is reaching out, with pardon and with saving power, even where these are least deserved. And that is what we are somehow sure of when we remember Jesus—sure that "God was in Christ reconciling the world to himself."

Index